PLAY TIME IS OVER

By L. V. Perez Jr.

ISBN – 13:9780692290835

ISBN – 10:0692290834

TABLE OF CONTENTS

DEDICATION

The dedication of this book goes to the Lord Jesus Christ for His inspiration, wisdom, and direction, and I would like to also dedicate this book to my Mother Lee and three sons Nikolis, Christian, and Angel for their support and encouragement. I would like to acknowledge my grandparents Mirta and Anibal Rossello for their constant care of my three sons while I have been in pursuit of my call to the ministry and writing of this book! They have been a steady anchor during very rough seas. In addition to the team of editors Alberto De La Rosa, and Brenda Dennis you are a dream team. Also to all those who have problems dealing with fear or unbelief.

ACKNOWLEDGEMENTS

First, I must acknowledge My Lord Jesus Christ, and His most precious Holy Spirit without them in my life I am nothing; thank you for giving me the wisdom and direction when creating this book. In addition, I would like to thank all others that supported me, especially my mentors, and friends Apostle Luis Capdevila, Pastor Calvin Green and the whole family at New Covenant Ministry and Pastor John at Good Samaritan. I would also like to acknowledge my great family of phenomenal theologians such as Dr. Carlos N Marquez, and Dr. George Walters. My gratitude goes out to Dr Myles Munroe for his encouraging letters. In addition, I would like to thank Dr Rodney Howard Browne for the touch of anointing he released upon my life and for being a great Man of God that has stood for the things of God and protected his anointing. To all of my bible students at Mount Tabor Bible College, I thank you for you support as well. May the Lord develop you for His purpose, knowing all of you has been a tremendous source of motivation in my life.

PLAY TIME IS OVER

Introduction

This book is an in depth look on events that took place on 9/11 the day of infamy. When the United States was suddenly attacked by terrorists, who hijacked airplanes. I will show the exact place in the Bible that had this day of horrific events. Afterwards, you will see it with your own eyes; you will say this is too much to be a coincidence. You will see verse-by-verse proofed from the time the airplanes left their airports to the time they hit the targets. You will also see the daily events of 9/11 came in the same order just as the verse spoke of it happening. This book will also give you pictures to show you what was taking place at that particular time. Like I said you're really going to see it from another perspective. It was the day that shook America and put us on our knees. We will see that every stock that was listed in the World Trade Center was also listed in the verses of the Bible and they were identical. You will also see that three times it tell us in one hour "your doom has come" and in one hour all three events took place; from when the airplanes took off, until they hit the Towers and Pentagon as well as it told us "in one day your destruction will come." I will go into deep detail showing the times all planes left and when the crashes took place as well the time both towers came down to the very second that the stock market crashed. It only took one day for all of this to take place from the stock market crashing to the towers collapsing. Then you will see events that have been taking place around the world like earthquakes and what Jesus said would happen in the last days. You will see over a ten to twenty year period of earthquakes that hit the earth and how they have been gradually intensifying. In addition, you find in this book an end time scenario about the last days of the United States, and who could be America's next leader and I will take you verse by verse so you can see, where America might be headed. Then there is a chapter where I show you the essence of time and why we should use what little time we have left to glorify God and do His will. Because time is running out for us, we are living in the end times. In addition, this book has a chapter leading those to true repentance and breaking down really the grace that God called us to live in. You will get an in depth look on how God looks at you and how he really loves you. After you see the love, He has for you it will be easy to repent. Remember, the character of God is love; He is not the big bad God that wants to hurt you or tell you about your imperfections. The Bible tells us with love and kindness have I drawth thee. In the book of Romans it tells us (Rom 2:4) "Or despisest thou the riches of his goodness and forbearance and longsuffering; not knowing that the goodness of God leadeth thee to repentance?" God is a good Father that loves us and wants the very best for us in all things. This book also goes into detail about being Spirit filled and why it so important to invite the Holy Spirit into your life. The book of Revelation says that God will give the devil the power of free reign for a certain amount of time. It goes into detail why someone, that has never asked to be filled with the Holy Spirit, is in danger of being possessed by evil spirits in these last days. In addition, this book teaches you how to invite the Holy Spirit in your life and how to be filled by the Spirit of the Almighty God. The last part of this book has the word of God and His promises; I give you scriptures to stand on; therefore giving you strength to look at or do a daily reflection to remind yourselves of the promises of God. Many of theologians have said there is over 300 promises in the Bible. How many have you claimed? Now is the time to claim everything that the devil took from you, your peace, joy, health, happiness, abundant living and destiny. Come let us search together and find the truth and the truth shall set you free and whosoever the son sets free is free indeed.

CHAPTER 1

Play Time Is Over

I was reading the book of Psalms one day, the 22nd song of Psalm to be exact, when the spirit of the Lord began to speak to me concerning the attacks that took place on 9/11. He told me to go to the book of Revelation Ch. 18 and as I read it, the spirit of the Lord began to give an in-depth look on what happen on the day of 9/11. He began from the first verse; it was one of the scariest times of my life. The first verse reads like this:

(Rev 18:1)

> *"After this I saw another angel coming down from heaven. He had great authority, and the earth was illuminated by his splendor."*

The angel that came down brought forth illumination-meaning light. The King James Bible says the earth was lit up by His splendor which is the whole earth meaning all nations saw what happen that day. Because of the news and media and TV or computer; the whole world, took a part of those events as well as the United States. The first verse states that "after this I saw another angel coming down" so there had to be more than one angel that John saw because he uses the word 'another'. The word another in Greek means **"allos"** which means more than one" There were three targets that were hit that day. The first two were the Twin Towers known as the World Trade Center and the third target was the Pentagon. The 2nd verse got my attention because it says the word fallen twice and two towers fell.

(Rev 18:2)

"And he cried mightily with a strong voice, saying, Babylon the great is fallen, is fallen, and is become the habitation of devils, and the hold of every foul spirit, and a cage of every unclean and hateful bird."

It's amazing that it describes birds in the verse and to someone in John's age a plane would probably look as a bird. The verse also says it has become habitation of devils and the hold of every foul spirit. Foul spirits of greed lust, murder, coveting, envy, idolaters, hate, homosexuality and deception in general infects this country. Those spirits have already entered our atmosphere in the United States. Let's look at where the attacks were successful; Washington D.C where corruption takes root from unjust laws that are raping the American people of their rights by imposing unfair higher taxes on them and imposing unfair laws to help the rich get tax breaks. They have also agreed to allow abortion to take place and are trying desperately to implement a law that will let homosexuals have rights to marry. These are two things; the Bible says are an abomination to God. Also, New York a place that houses over two million Jews (Gods chosen people), which the Muslims hate, and wish they can exterminate. New York has also allowed all types of greed, crime and a turn the other cheek policy when it comes to moral issues, like crime and gay rights. As long as you have the money to pay for the laws that you want to be enforced they have no problem with it. Christianity is too far tolerant on these issues and not many churches have the tenacity or zeal to preach the true gospel of Christ, which is repentance, love, and grace of our Lord Jesus. However, if you notice these two locations were the only ones that got hit every other attack was folded. Now verse three gets deep into why the wrath of the Lord was upon them.

(Rev 18:3)

"For all the nations have drunk the maddening wine of her adulteries. The kings of the earth committee adultery with her, and the merchants of the earth grew rich from her excessive luxuries."

Like I said, all nations deal with both New York City and Washington D.C. Both have become rich from her excessive luxuries. The definition of a merchant is one who buys and sells commodities for profit or deals and trade goods. Now I know the World Trade Center was our stock exchange, but not just ours meaning the people of the United States only, it was for every nation of the world, which is why it was called The World Trade Center. This is why I believe John speaks that all nations have drunk the maddening wine. The word *maddening* is only used in NIV bible and it means driving to madness but in the Greek it is written differently it says: *"For of the wine of the wrath of fornication her have drunk."* The word <u>wrath</u> appears and the Lord gave <u>wrath</u> because their sin has reached the heavens. As you read the book of Revelation you will notice where the wrath of God will be poured out: (Rev 16:1) ***Then I heard a loud voice from the temple saying to the seven angels, "Go, pour out the seven bowls of God's wrath on the earth."*** The scripture is very clear on whose wrath is being poured out on the earth, it is God's wrath. Is there another being in the bible that can give an order to an Angel other than God? As John points out in the latter. The next verse seems like a call from God for the saints to come out of her before his wrath takes place.

(Rev 18:4)

"Then I heard another voice from heaven say: "Come out of her, my people, so that you will not share in her sins, so that you will not receive any of her plagues;"

If you notice this is a call to the saints from The Lord. I found something else very interesting that took place on 9/11/01. I heard a Man of God by the name of Perry Stone preach, on the events that took place on that day. He said that a church that was located across the street from the towers had a total of one hundred and fifty members of their church working at the World Trade Center. It just so happen, that they did not go into work on that day. Some reported to their pastor that they did not get up on time, some had their car break down, and others didn't feel like working that day. I do not find that surprising to me at all because the Lord warned Noah of destruction of a flood that was to come in the book of Genesis. God protects his people, if you do not think so just read the whole Book of Psalms, especially Psalms 91. It goes a little like this! (Ps 91:1-8) *"He who dwells in the shelter of the Most High will rest in the shadow of the Almighty. 2 I will say of the LORD, "He is my refuge and my fortress, my God, in whom I trust." 3 Surely he will save you from the fowler's snare and from the deadly pestilence. 4 He will cover you with his feathers, and under his wing you will find refuge; his faithfulness will be your shield and rampart. 5 You will not fear the terror of night, nor the arrow that flies by day, 6 nor the pestilence that stalks in the darkness, nor the plague that destroys at midday. 7 A thousand may fall at your side, ten thousand at your right hand, but it will not come near you. 8 You will only observe with your eyes and see the punishment of the wicked."* As you can see, He will protect you from deadly pestilence or terror. The word pestilence means (*deber*) *in Hebrew, which means murrain, pestilence, plague,* disease *and sickness.* The word used in the four verses of Revelation is plague this means (*plege*) *in Greek meaning: a stroke; by implication, a wound; figuratively, a calamity: plague, stripe, wound (-ed).* As you can see the word plague does not have to mean diseases, it also means a stroke; by implication, a wound, or calamity. Definitely, a wound and calamity came by these attacks on 9/11. People were terrified and wounded emotionally and physically. The victims of 9/11 had loved ones desperately hoping that they would be a survivor in the most horrific time in American history. The day of 9/11 was like that of the day when God lifted the hedge of protection off of Jobs household in one day and destruction came swiftly. The fifth verse reminded me of what the Lord told Solomon, for the sake of my servant David the Lord did not destroy a city called Judah. (2 Kings 8:19) *"Nevertheless, for the sake of his servant David, the LORD was not willing to destroy Judah. He had promised to maintain a lamp for David and his descendants forever."* The fifth verse tells us that the people's sin has reached the heavens so let's go there.

(Rev 18:5)

" for her sins are piled up to heaven, and God has remembered her crimes."

Jesus said so as in the days of Noah so shall it be in the last times (Luke 17:26, 27)

"Just as it was in the days of Noah, so also will it be in the days of the Son of Man. People were eating; drinking, marrying and being given in marriage up to the day Noah entered the ark. Then the flood came and destroyed them all." Why has God lifted His hand of protection off of us, because we allow gays to have rights by marrying each other, even though it has been voted against hundreds of times. We allow the rich to exploit the poor with unreasonable taxes and laws, we partake in abortion which is murder in Gods eyes. We have Pastors in churches all over the United States that preach complete heresy and don't want to preach the true Gospel of Christ, which is the grace of our Lord, and teach us His love for us. We worship money, as it was God himself, we commit adultery as if it's a daily ritual and practice divorce. Marriage is a covenant oath under God and we treat it just as if it is a date that went wrong. Maybe this is what John meant when he said "your sin has piled up to heaven." We allow the spirit of greed to come in like never before just as all the others empires before us. Just as the Roman Empire fell because of that same spirit so did Persian, Grecian, Babylonian and Egyptian. They all fell to the spirit of greed and pride. We need to learn from the history books so we do not fall as they did, we need to humble ourselves and turn from our wicked ways and then and only then will God hear us and heal our land. (2 Chron 7:14)*" if my people, who are called by my name, will humble themselves and pray and seek my face and turn from their wicked ways, then will I hear from heaven and will forgive their sin and will heal their land."*

It is very clear in the last days God will bestow His wrath upon the ungodly. 9/11 was a wakeup call, for those who do not believe in the mighty hand of a sovereign God. I would like to ask a question? How many of the same individuals that show up in churches months after 9/11 still attend church today? Have they found themselves under a false sense of protection; that this government can protect them because the America government thus far has stopped all other attacks? Remember the end of that verse say God has remembered her crimes; maybe its the crimes of us not remembering Him, by taking prayer and the Ten Commandments out of schools and letting them teach children sexual education or evolution. Alternatively, maybe its letting Muslims alter Christian holidays for their religion's purposes. Could we even have a church in a Muslim country or tell them their mosque offends us, No you could not! Why, because they behead infidels in their country! That means anyone that's not of the Muslim religion. Then I began to read the sixth verse, and the Lord began to show me deeper and deeper revelation of the events of 9/11 come lets go there.

(Rev 18:6)

"Reward her even as she rewarded you, and double unto her double according to her works: in the cup which she hath filled fill to her double."

As I was reading the word "double" stood out to me then the Lord spoke and said how many buildings were hit, my reply was three the South Tower, the North Tower and the Pentagon. That's why John wrote the three double's in the verse. In the King James Version, the three doubles appear even in the Greek but the NIV bible drop out one of the doubles. I believe the Holy Spirit wanted those three doubles in there for this reason. The seventh and eight verses stood out as well. I saw how verse upon verse was unfolding and it became scary to me. Why is He showing me this and no one else? Someone with media connections, someone that could get the word to a broad range of people can warn them. I was a baby Christian at that time, what can I do with this information? The next two verses hit me as if a ton of bricks had fell off a roof. I began to be in mourning for the people that were lost and wondered if they knew our Lord Jesus and if they even had a chance to meet Him. Some people I saw were jumping out of windows because of the fires on their floor had trapped them, did they know the Lord I wonder? Did they read the story of the three Hebrew boys that were thrown in a fiery furnace because king Nebuchadnezzar told them if they would not worship the image of gold he had set up, he was going to burn them to death. (Dan 3:19-21) Did they know that Shadrach, Meshach and Abednego after being put in the fiery furnace did not get burned, nor did they smell of smoke they came out untouched?

(Dan 3:27) He saw that the fire had not harmed their bodies, nor was a hair of their heads singed; their robes were not scorched, and there was no smell of fire on them.

It's unbelievable what kind a God we serve. How can you be in the fire and not even so much as a hair on your head be touched? Today the best thing to do in those circumstances is get on your knees and pray protect me father, do not give up just speak to your circumstance. If Ezekiel can prophesy dry bones back to life and Joshua can stop time with a prayer, what can you do? Remember He is no respecter of person; that means if He did for them He do it for you. The next two verses go into deep detail of the events and deal with the plagues and the fire because the towers were consumed by fire, let's go there.

(Rev 18:7-8)

7 How much she hath glorified herself, and lived deliciously, so much torment and sorrow give her: for she saith in her heart, I sit a queen, and am no widow, and shall see no sorrow. 8 Therefore shall her plagues come in one day, death, and mourning, and famine; and she shall be utterly burned with fire: for strong is the Lord God who judgeth her.

The eighth verse says therefore her plagues will overtake her in one day; the destruction of the World Trade Center happened in one day. The destruction of the country's financial solutions happened in one day. Remember the word plagues means a stroke; by implication, a wound, or calamity now the picture is getting a little clear. Now let's finish the verse. It says her plagues will come in one day and it lists those plagues. Death is the first thing that took place that day. Why do I say that? I say this because the people on the planes died on impact, also people were jumping out of windows as well. Then the next plague that took place that day is mourning. We the people of the United States were in mourning for the people in the planes and buildings but most of the whole world was in mourning not because of American casualties; it was because there stocks and money were in those building. Remember the name of the building? The World Trade Center! That is where all nations came to trade. The third plague was famine. Now let's look into what type of famines took place that day. The first famine was for the people trapped in the buildings. Once they collapsed; the people were trapped without food or water for days. The second famine was for the United States because the stock market crashed that day as well and the United States went in economic crisis. When you say the word famine people always often think about food or water; never money. However, the word famine means shortage of anything. Now lets take even a closer look at what took place. First it says that plagues would consume her in one day and it did. It lists the three plagues: death, mourning, and famine and it is in that exact order that they happened. That's too much to be a coincidence don't you think? Than it says, she will be consumed by fire and that is exactly how the tower were consumed. Fire caused the towers to collapse. Because of the heat the metal was weakened and caused the structure to give way.

(Rev18:8) she shall be utterly burned with fire: for strong is the Lord God who judgeth her.

The next verse is self-explaining. It exclaims that the kings of the earth will see the smoke and weep over her. Like I said before, they are not worried about American casualties, they're worried about their riches. They see their bank account going up in smoke. There is a picture from the smoke that came from the Towers that day, and it was amazing. It looks like the whole world could see it.

(Rev 18:9)

"When the kings of the earth who committed adultery with her and shared her luxury see the smoke of her burning, they will weep and mourn over her."

Then the tenth verse broke the revelations of these events wide open to me. It was like the Holy Spirit took off my blinders and I could see clear. The tenth verse put me on my knees asking the Lord why. He guided me and carried me through scripture as one in thought like never before, asking me questions so I would know right where to look. It was His research not mine. Let us look at the ten verses together shall we.

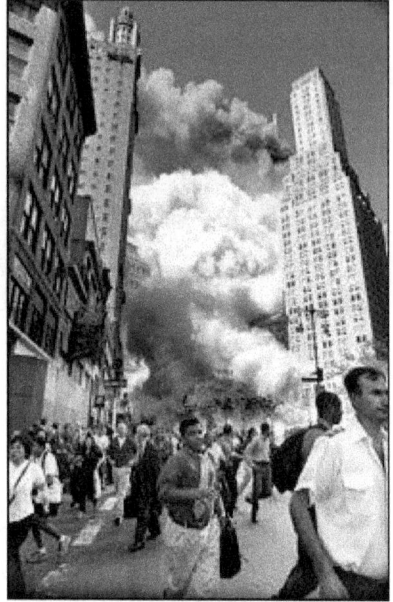

(Rev 18:10)

"Terrified at her torment, they will stand far off and cry: "'Woe! Woe, O great city,

O Babylon, city of power! In one hour your doom has come!"

Now we are going to take a deep look on the events of 9/11, which took place that day. The scripture say "in one hour your doom has come." On the 8am, American Airlines flight 11, a Boeing 767 departs Boston bound for Los Angeles. On 8:14am, United Airlines flight 175 a

Boeing 767 departs from Boston Logan Airport bound for Los Angeles. On 8:21am American Airlines flight 77, a Boeing 757 departs Washington Dulles airport bound for Los Angeles. Lets take a deeper look at this. All airplanes took off within one hour of each other the first one was at (8:00am flight 11) the second at (8:14am flight 175) and the third at (8:21am flight 77) This really got my attention because this is to much to be a coincidence. The verse tells us in one hour your doom has come and all flights took off in the same hour but it doesn't end here it gets deeper and deeper. Come lets go there together. The 11,12 and13 verses offer a deeper Revelation into the heart of the World Trade Center operation. What is that goes on within these Towers to get so many threats or foiled attacks? Because this was not the first terrorist attack on the World Trade Center! Those verses tell us the very function of those towers, let's go there.

(Rev 18:11-13)

11 "The merchants of the earth will weep and mourn over her because no one buys their cargoes any more- 12 cargoes of gold, silver, precious stones and pearls; fine linen, purple, silk and scarlet cloth; every sort of citron wood, and articles of every kind made of ivory, costly wood, bronze, iron and marble; 13 cargoes of cinnamon and spice, of incense, myrrh and frankincense, of wine and olive oil, of fine flour and wheat; cattle and sheep; horses and carriages; and bodies and souls of men.

Now remember we talked about the definition of a merchant. A merchant is defined as one who buys and sells commodities for profit or deals and trades goods. Sounds like a stockbroker takes a look at the list of cargoes and it says no one will be able to buy them anymore. Since 9/11/01 has anyone bought anything from the World Trade Center? No. Why because scriptures cannot be broken. Look how long it has been since that happened and furthermore; they haven't broke ground to build a new facility! My Bible says they will not because this is a prophecy movement and prophecy must be fulfilled. Jesus himself said that (Matt 5:18) *"I tell you the truth, until heaven and earth disappear, not the smallest letter, not the least stroke of a pen, will by any means disappear from the Law until everything is accomplished."* Now let's look at the cargoes. This is interesting I say this because it lists every stock to the last one to the T. These are stocks that the World Trade Center dealt in and when you see the words "horses and carriages", how many people know that Wells Fargo bank lists as one of the stocks in the New York Stock exchange. Well guess what their emblem is, horses pulling a carriage. Then it goes deeper, the verse says the word <u>bodies</u> and bodies were found and souls of men were judged. Why would bodies and souls of men be listed with stocks that happen to be in buildings that collapsed? Well we know as Christians souls are judged at the point of death and if someone dies its their body they leave behind but their soul goes up to be judged.

(Rev18:13) and bodies and souls of men

This is very interesting to me why this Man of God would put stocks or in his time, called cargoes in the same place where bodies and soul of men that happen to be founded in the same place. This is intriguing to me and too much to be a so-called accident or by chance in the words of atheists that do not believe in a Sovereign God. The 14th verse says that never again the riches and splendor would be recovered and guess what they have not since this has happen.

(Rev 18:14)

"They will say, 'The fruit you longed for is gone from you. All your riches and splendor have vanished, never to be recovered.'

The next three verses are about how the merchants were weeping; of course, they would weep, it's a natural human response when something terrible like that happens. Nevertheless, are they weeping just because their riches went up in smoke or was there a sense of repentance that took place? My guess is there was no weeping asking God why did this happen or even weeping for all the massive casualties of the people that were loss. Many single parents died on 9/11. Were they weeping for a child that has no one to love them now? Because they loss the only person that cares for them; did they take responsibility for their action by getting on their knees asking the Lord for His forgiveness? Not to mention all the other people whom loss siblings and spouses to this great tragedy. Was there a sense of sorrow for what took place or was it to easy to point the finger and place blame on Osama bin Laden? The earlier verses in revelations 18 tell us, we should point the finger at ourselves because it says in the 2nd verse she has become a home for demons. If you read through the whole Bible you will notice every time Israel turned their back on God it was a remedy for disaster. Then the 17th verse hit me again like a wave of Glorious revelation from the shock. It was overwhelming and the Lord asked me yet another question to my amazement this is too much to be a coincidence. Let's go there together verses 15-17.

(Rev 18:15-17)

15 The merchants who sold these things and gained their wealth from her will stand far off, terrified at her torment. They will weep and mourn

16 and cry out: "'Woe! Woe, O great city, dressed in fine linen, purple and scarlet,

and glittering with gold, precious stones and pearls!

17 In one hour such great wealth has been brought to ruin!'

Verse 17 stood out to me, then the Lord asked me, what times did all three planes crash?

So I began to research it, I know all three took off in the same hour but to my surprise, all crashes happen within one hour of taking off as well, let's go there together and see. We know flight 11 took off at 8am but did you know it crashed into the north tower at 8:45am and this verse rang out to me *"In one hour such great wealth has been brought to ruin!'* Let's look at flight 175 remember it took off at 8:14am and crash into the south tower at 9:02am that is within one hour of take-off, again the verse rang out to me. *In one hour such great wealth has been brought to ruin!* The third flight was flight 77 it took off at 8:21am and it crashed into the pentagon at 9:41am that was 21 minutes off, then I asked the Lord what happened. Then He spoke and said this flight did not crash within an hour because the target did not have great wealth, the verse says *"In one hour such great wealth has been brought to ruin!"* The pentagon does not have any commodity of wealth at all. However, He said let's look again at what time all three flights crashed the first one was at 8:45am the second 9:02am and third at

9:41am, all three flights crashed within one hour of each other. "*In one hour such great wealth has been brought to ruin!*" It even goes deeper than that at 9:32am that morning of 9/11 all financial markets in the United States were closed the stock market crashed within one hour of the planes hitting the towers. *In one hour such great wealth has been brought to ruin!*' The Lord began to speak to me again and asked me where were all three planes headed I look and found out something I did not notice before. All three planes were headed to Los Angeles the word Los Angeles means *City of the Angels*. Remember the *1st verse* which said *"I saw another angel coming down from heaven and the earth was illuminated by his splendor"* this is to much to be a coincidence. All three planes were scheduled to land in the City of the Angels. Maybe those are the angels that took off the protection for those planes, which lead them to their destruction. The verse 17 also says that every sea captain and all who earn their living from the sea could see the smoke of her burning 17,18 verses. This is what exactly took place for all those that were on ships that were in the harbor and far away at sea.

(Rev18:17-18)

"In one hour such great wealth has been brought to ruin!'

"Every sea captain, and all who travel by ship, the sailors, and all who earn their living from the sea, will stand far off. When they see the smoke of her burning, they will exclaim, 'Was there ever a city like this great city?'

As you can clearly see the smoke from the Towers went up and was seen for miles and miles. From the sea you could see the destruction; even from the ocean it was easily seen by all that made their living by sea according to scripture. Nevertheless, verse 19 went yet deeper again. Let's go there together.

(Rev 18:19)

"They will throw dust on their heads, and with weeping and mourning cry out:

"'Woe! Woe, O great city, where all who had ships on the sea, became rich through her

wealth! In one hour she has been brought to ruin!"

Now I'm thinking, is there an event that day that happened in one hour that I missed. The Lord responded yes. He spoke and asked "what times did the building collapse?" I began searching and found something very interesting that took place. *Flight 11 crashes into the north tower at 8:47am; 10:28am the tower completely collapses. At 9:02am flight 175 crashes into the south tower; at 9:50am, the south tower collapses.* The south tower was hit second but was the first to collapse, then the Lord had reminded me of the meeting between the Secret Service officer in the classroom of second-grade class with President Bush. It was Andrew Card, who whispers in the ear of the President that an airplane had struck the towers and the reply from President Bush seemed odd to me. He asked if the south tower was hit, I wonder why He was worried about the south not the north tower until I had a conversation that took place with my cousin, which is a retired Secret Service agent. He explained to me that the north tower collected data and the south tower stored the data. If they lose the south tower, the stock market would be lost. Now let's take a close look at this; *the south tower was hit at 9:02am* and *collapses at 9:50am* and the *stock market crashed at 9:32* am. Let's look at the 19 verse just one more time *"'Woe! Woe, O great city, where all who had ships on the sea, became rich through her wealth! In one hour she has been brought to ruin!"* In one hour, all this took place! The stock market was closed 18 minutes before the south tower collapses. It's time for America to repent from their wicked ways and ask the Lord to come back into their hearts as the word of the Lord says; "If my people will turn from their wicked way then I will hear from heaven and heal their land. The next two verses brought a powerful end and conclusion, to a rude awakening go there with me.

(Rev 18:20-21)

"Rejoice over her, O heaven! Rejoice, saints and apostles and prophets!

God has judged her for the way she treated you.'" *Then a mighty angel picked up a boulder the size of a large millstone and threw it into the sea, and said: "With such violence the great city of Babylon will be thrown down, never to be found again"*

The verse explains a mighty angel picked up a boulder the size of a large millstone and threw it into the sea, and said: "With such violence the great city of Babylon will be thrown down, never to be found again. The words rang out aloud to me as if an angel came down to tell me; hey, this was an act of violence that caused this to take place. *"With such violence the great city of Babylon will be thrown down, never to be found again."* It was about six months after the 9/11/01 attacks when the Lord showed me this revelation. It has been over ten years now; one decade has gone by and now it's being released. As a warning to not forget the day of wrath and destruction that came in one hour. The rest of Revelation tells much of the same thing; never will music or joy be heard in it ever again. I'm not going into great detail because I believe there is still another attack on the horizon that will complete the chapter 18 of revelation by John, given of our Lord Jesus Christ.

CHAPTER 2

Recalling the Mystery of the Towers & the Time

Let's take a look at all the events that took place on 9/11/01 and how they coincide with one another. I will find it hard to believe even an atheist, would say all this that happened was only by coincidence. The first verse says I saw another angel come from heaven and you have all three airplanes taking off that were hijacked going to Los Angeles which means "city of the angels." Then Revelation 18 tells us in the second verse, fallen, fallen and two towers fell by a terrorist attack, it exclaims in the three verses that nations grew rich through her. The fourth verse is a warning for the saints to leave her. As I said before, there were churches located in front of the World Trade Center and one of them was named St. Nicholas church which was totally destroyed. I do not know if the members were from that particular church, however one of the churches had 150 members not showing up for work on the day of 9/11. The six verses use the word double three times in the Greek and King James Bible. I found that to be interesting because three targets were hit which were the Twin Towers and Pentagon. The eighth verse tells about the plagues she would receive in one day. Now note all this took place in one day and it also goes into deep detail explaining to us. First came Death, Mourning and Famine and they came in the same exact order as John prophesied. Then the same verse exclaims fire and the Towers collapsing due to being consumed by fire. Fires consume her and fire is what causes them to collapse. The ninth verse says when the kings of the earth see her smoke of her burning they would weep and mourn. They did, not because of American casualties; they were worried about their own personal finances. However, the tenth verse goes in deep; it says in one hour your doom has come and all three airplanes left in the same hour. The eleventh verse through fifteen verses spoke of the merchandise that the World Trade Center traded in and list every stock to the smallest detail that was in those buildings. It also tells us that bodies and souls of men would be recovered and they were. Guess what, there many bodies found and souls are judged at the point of death, that is what the book of Ecclesiastes exclaims it says. (Eccl 12:6-7) *"Remember him-before the silver cord is severed, or the golden bowl is broken; before the pitcher is shattered at the spring, or the wheel broken at the well, and the dust returns to the ground it came from, and the spirit returns to God who gave it."* The last part tells us clearly that the spirit of a man returns to God who gave it, means death this is the point of judgment for man. On top of that, in verse nineteen; all Airplanes crash in one hour of each other, both south tower and stock market crashed within a one-hour as well. The verse stated in one hour great wealth would be brought to ruin and it did. There were total of three places in Revelation 18 where it says in one hour and all three happen. Now is the time for America to repent for all that she has done and go back to serving a mighty God. Time is one of the most precious commodities that man has to deal with because of the devil and man's disobedience. Time itself was never created for man in the beginning, it was created for the vegetation and plants and the earth in (Gen1: 14) I say this only because man was created to live forever. When Adam disobeyed God, that is when time became a part of the curse for him, time became relevant too him. It started with a tree that time itself was established in the beginning that became a part of him. As soon as

Adam partook of the fruit, time became a part of him and entered his DNA. This is how sin effects our lives- once being contaminated; the residue stays with you and the consequence of it comes upon you. Thank you Jesus for taking the consequence for us and from us. (Time) Came forth to man forever upon the earth because of sin and disobedience. God created Adam to live forever being that (Gen 3:22) clearly states that. Why would time mean anything to a person that is immortal? It would not! Because they would have all the time in the world to accomplish what ever task or dream they wanted; therefore not having a sense of urgency of getting left behind. Time is the one thing people judge success by. How long did it take you to finish school or to get a promotion at work? Or how long before your ministry took before it grew? People always find ways of competing with one another by using time as the residing factor. The only thing we are suppose to use time for is to serve and worship the Lord our God; because all of us know that a man is only given a certain amount of time on this earth. When our Father says your time is up its up! Death comes rushing in and death cares nothing of the time you spent here and its main function is to stop your time on this earth. God is the only one that can intervene on your behalf as He did with Hezekiah and stop time. *(Isa 38:2)* *"Hezekiah turned his face to the wall and prayed to the LORD."* Moreover, the Bible says the Lord granted him fifteen more years. The Lord also heard a man by the name of Joshua pray to stop time and granted his request as well. The sun did not go down until the nation of Israel avenged itself on its enemies. (Josh 10:13-14) *"So the sun stood still, and the moon stopped, till the nation avenged itself on its enemies, as it is written in the Book of Jashar. The sun stopped in the middle of the sky and delayed going down about a full day. There has never been a day like it before or since, a day when the LORD listened to a man. Surely the LORD was fighting for Israel!"* The bible clearly states that the God who created time can also stop time. People do not realize that the very day Jesus died on the cross He stopped time for them. Time went from B.C to A.D. He also took death from us as well through His Love, grace and mercy. It is our time now saints of God, what are we going to do with it from this day forth? Are we going to keep wasting it? Are, we going to cherish every moment of it and thank the Lord for giving us the time we do have and to make it right for Him? Now is the time saints to get on our knees and thank Jesus for the very breath we have. It could have been us that met destruction swiftly. How many times have you been in a narrow escape with your life and did not even acknowledge Him for keeping you? Let's look at it this way; the Lord gave Hezekiah fifteen more years to live. How about if you knew you only had fifteen years to live? Would you waste time or would every second of every day count to you? Would you thank Him for every second He gave you and hope only to please Him; the one who gave you more time? The bible tells us to give thanks to Him in all things. Do you thank Him for putting food on your table or gas in your car and a roof over your head? You still have time to do so, all you have to do is say "Lord Jesus thank you for your protection and all that you provide me, thank you for the job I have, and the car I drive and all the food I eat every day, thank you Father." He smiles upon the very ones that acknowledge Him, believe me it's not a waste of time; it is the mere essence of why we exist. He created man to please Him; not to please himself. That is where we waste so much of our time; trying to please ourselves and never fulfilling that dream because without Jesus you are wasting your time. There will always be a hole in you that needs to be filled. Some of the richest people in the world commit suicide because they believe they can buy their way to happiness. Once achieving it; they still find out there is still a big hole in them needing to be filled and the only way to fill it, is by a person named Jesus. How many people waste valuable time try to become rich? They believe money is going to be the answer to all their problems. They need to do a little history check on the world's richest people. They will find out they were miserable people and 80% of them committed suicide. So let's put an emphasis about wasting time on self pleasure instead of His pleasure. When you find out what our Father has for your life, you will fill the void that's in your life with joy. Pure joy will come inside you. There is a song that says this little light of mine I'm going to let it shine, let it shine, let it shine. The joy that He gives you is more precious than gold, rubies or pearls. It can't be replaced by any materialistic thing on the earth so stop wasting your time. This is the joy and peace that will come over you. Jesus said, "Peace I leave with you" this is His promise to you.(John 14:25-27) *"All this I have spoken while still with you. But the Counselor, the Holy Spirit, whom the Father will send in my name, will teach you all things and will remind you of everything I have said to you. Peace I leave with you; my peace I give you. I do not give to you as the world gives. Do not let your hearts be troubled and do not be afraid."*

CHAPTER 3

The Earth Is Running Out Of Time

The sermon the Lord gave me was about things that already have taken place in our world and how they relate to what is about to happen. I do not claim to be a prophet, I just have a responsibility to reveal what God has shown me and what He wants me to share, and besides; all of us are simply messengers.

In (Matthew 24: 4-7) Jesus said, "watch out that no one deceive you, for many will come in my name claiming I am the Christ and will deceive many. You will hear of wars and rumors of wars, but see to it that you are not alarmed, for such things must take place, but that is not yet the end. For nation will rise against nation, and kingdom against kingdom and in various place there will be famines and earthquakes. But these things are merely the beginning of birth pains."

The word "famine" of course means shortage. The United States is going through an economic famine. The price of oil has skyrocketed because of oil shortages. Jesus also said there would be earthquakes. There has been an earthquake every year since the tsunami and earthquake in India on December 26, 2004. More than 225,000 people in 11 countries were affected, with the inundating coastal communities with waves up to 30 miles and 100 feet. It was one of the deadliest natural disasters in history. Indonesia Sri Lanka, India, and Thailand were the hardest hit with a magnitude between 9.1 and 9.3. It was the second largest quake ever recorded on a seismograph. This earthquake had the longest duration of faulting ever observed, between 8.3 and 10 minutes, it caused the entire planet to vibrate as much as 1cm-0.5 inches. It triggered another earthquake as far as Alaska. The most recent ones were in Haiti, that claimed 316,000 lives on January 12, 2010 and in Japan, March 11, 2011 that claimed 20,352 lives this year.

If you go to (Revelations 16:18) it reads, *" then there came flashes of lightning sounds and peals of thunder and there was a great earthquake, "such as there had not been since man came to be upon the earth, so great an earthquake was it, and so mighty."*

Scientist now believe that the moon is drifting farther from the earth because of this earthquake. No earthquake like that has ever occurred since man has been on the earth, so tremendous was that quake. Scientists believe the moon is drifting farther from the earth and due to that quake, they also believe our days, will shorten because of this. Let's take a look at the book of Matthew and see what Jesus said about the end times.

(Matthew 24:21-22) says that, "for then there will be great distress unequaled from the beginning of the world until now and never to be equal again". The 22nd verse says, "If those days have not been cut short no one would survive, but for the sake of the elect those days will be shorten".

I found that very interesting because Jesus said, "If those days have not been cut short no one would survive, but for the sake of the elect those days will be shortened." Because scientists are telling us that if the moon stays its course by drifting off, it will cause our days to shorten bringing this scripture into fulfillment. What did he mean by such a statement? Well let's look at it from his prospective, Jesus knows all things and one of those things spoke about by Him and by prophets was astronomical signs. As you can see, this verse stood out for me. The 29th verse states that *"immediately after the distress of those days, the sun will be dark in and the moon will not give its light, the stars will fall from the sky and the heavenly bodies will be shaken.* These astronomical signs are going to appear in the last days. This verse appears in ten other places in the Bible. In *Isaiah 13:10, Ezekiel 32:17, Joel 2:10, Joel 3:15, Luke 21: 25, Mark 13:24, Revelations 6:12/7:16/8:12.*

In these scriptures, the Lord has given us a small look at what will take place on the earth with visions of astronomical signs happening in the heavens. As you can see, many things are happening even as I am writing this. The earthquakes take on a significant role. Because of their magnitude; they have shaken the earth to it core, causing significant affects to our atmosphere. Let's look at how many earthquakes have hit since the big one in 2004. These are only the ones with major fatalities, in each year after 2004 there has been more than fifteen earthquakes a year.

On October 8th, 2005 in Pakistan, an earthquake hit killing 80,000 people with a magnitude 7.6

On October 5th, 2006, an earthquake hit and killed 78,000 people with a magnitude of 7.6.

On September 12th, 2007 an earthquake hit in Sumatra killing 25 people. It hit with a magnitude of 8.5

On May 8th, 2008 cyclone hit killing over 30,000 people.

Another earthquake hit in China on May 12th, 2008 had the magnitudes of 7.9.

The first reports said there were 10,000 casualties, but now they say casualties are up to 69,197 people.

On September 29th & September 30th 2009, two earthquakes hit the Samoa Islands with the strength of 7.5 and 8.1 magnitudes it claimed 1,115 lives.

The most recent one was in Haiti that claimed 316,000 lives in year 2012; it was a 7.1 magnitude. On January 12th, 2010 in Japan on March 11th, 2011 an earthquake that claimed 20,352 lives had a magnitude of 9.0. As you can see the earth is beginning the birth pains, that Jesus talked about.

(Matt 24:7-8) *"Nation will rise against nation, and kingdom against kingdom. There will be famines and earthquakes in various places. All these are the beginning of birth pains."*

All those signs are taking place and as we speak, we have seen nation rise against nation. There are famines occurring not only in the United States, but also in other nations along with job shortages. In addition, around the world with food and jobs there are more and more people on unemployment in this country since before the last 70 years. It is almost getting to be a depression as it happened before. The Bible states this will be the beginning of birth pains. In (Matt 24:8) in the King James Bible it states the word sorrows. In the Greek, it means (odin) *a pang or throe, especially of childbirth: pain, sorrow, and travail.* During pain a woman goes into labor; before she delivers the baby, water always breaks and as Pastor Stone believes, that is why we are having so many hurricanes. During the moment of travail, the woman's water breaks and then she gives birth. Therefore, as you can see the earth itself is going to tribulation with different catastrophic events. Therefore, God only knows what's on the horizon for our planet earth, only God knows when and where all things will take place. Jesus told us that in His words.

(Matt 24:36-37) *"No one knows about that day or hour, not even the angels in heaven, nor the Son, but only the Father. As it was in the days of Noah, so it will be at the coming of the Son of Man."* However, the Bible says those that truly believe will be saved; therefore it all comes down to do you believe? Nevertheless, be of good cheer and know today your Father will never leave you nor forsake you because He loves you. (1 Chron 28:20) *"And David said to his son Solomon, "Be strong and of good courage, and do it; do not fear nor be dismayed, for the LORD God—my God—will be with you. He will not leave you nor forsake you, until you have finished all the work for the service of the house of the LORD."* If He did not forsake Paul the one who murdered Christians for the sake of his own belief, and he did not leave Peter the one who denied him three times, Be of good cheer! There is a scripture, which tells us that nothing can separate us from the love of Christ. This is how much God loves you. He sends his very best for you to die as one of us, it tells us that in the book of Romans.

(Rom 8:32-39)

He who did not spare his own Son, but gave him up for us all-how will he not also, along with him, graciously give us all things? 33 Who will bring any charge against those whom God has chosen? It is God who justifies. 34 Who is he that condemns? Christ Jesus, who died-more than that, who was raised to life-is at the right hand of God and is also interceding for us. 35 Who shall separate us from the love of Christ? Shall trouble or hardship or persecution or famine or nakedness or danger or sword? 36 As it is written: "For your sake we face death all day long; we are considered as sheep to be slaughtered." 37 No, in all these things we are more than conquerors through him who loved us. 38 For I am convinced that neither death nor life, neither angels nor demons, neither the present nor the future, nor any powers, 39 neither height nor depth, nor anything else in all creation, will be able to separate us from the love of God that is in Christ Jesus our Lord.

David said it the best that he would not fear because the Lord thy God will protect him and keep him. Don't be afraid, know that God is all powerful. He is the one that created the Heavens and the earth so he knows how all things work.

(Ps 46:2-5)

" Therefore we will not fear, though the earth give way and the mountains fall into the heart of the sea, though its waters roar and foam and the mountains quake with their surging. Selah, There is a river whose streams make glad the city of God, the holy place where the Most High dwells. God is within her, she will not fall; God will help her at break of day."

Trust me when I say this to you. In the book of Jeremiah 29:11 the Lord says I know the plans I have for you, plans to prosper you and not to harm you. He did not send His only son to die on a cross and to leave us hopeless and defenseless. He is a good God that loves us even when we make mistakes and fall short of the mark, He still looks down upon us with love. The only thing we are called to do in this life is believe that Jesus is a loving Great God, so wonderful that the earth could not contain Him. Think of it this way; no matter where you go on this planet, He sees you and knows the very essence of your inner most being. The very things you think are secret to you, He already knows. Every time you worry about a worldly issue, He knows all about them and even about the simple worries of life, like what do I wear today. There is nothing hidden under the sun that He has not already thought of, nothing can catch Him by surprise. It was His plan from the beginning of the earth. So, just believe from today on.

CHAPTER 4

A Time to Reflect

I would like to take you to a place in time called the future, which no one knows but a selected few, the ones God can really trust with it. Why do I say this? Because men have a way of being boasters of themselves, saying it was their wisdom not revelation from God. Men through ages have presented themselves as great philosophers, teachers, psychics and even the Messiah a chosen vessel for the people of their time. Look for examples such as Alexander the Great, Attila the Hun, King Nebuchadezzar and Hitler. They were chosen vessels to carry wisdom far beyond that of any other men of their time. Hitler to his people on numerous occasions was called the messiah, and a prophet of the people, people were mesmerized by his speeches and he thought of himself as the messiah of his people. Nevertheless, they found out after the war that he was not; he was just a boaster of himself. It is very easy to let popularity sway your feelings about yourself when people constantly praise you for being smart, it's to easy to get a big head and feel that you caused all this by yourself not God. So this is what I mean by saying that only a selected few and only a selected few can handle the responsibility of knowing the future. The Bible calls them prophets. However, try to understand that the Bible lets you know the future, but revelation only comes from God at an appointed time. Understanding is a key to unlocking heavenly wisdom hidden from other generations; that is what the book of Ephesians tells us. (Eph 3:3-5)

"That is, the mystery made known to me by revelation, as I have already written briefly. In reading this, then, you will be able to understand my insight into the mystery of Christ, which was not made known to men in other generations as it has now been revealed by the Spirit to God's holy apostles and prophets."

Therefore, it is a very exciting time because the mystery Paul is writing about is a person that died to give us grace. His name is Jesus, no longer do we have to live in a time of fear because Jesus told all his children do not fear for I am with you. He will protect us. He is also called a prophet in the Bible so understand that all that is going on right now he foretold long ago. In Matt 24. Jesus told His disciples all that was to come upon the earth and He told them "do not worry for all must happen until the end of time." So we will dig in to scripture a little to see if we are living in the last days before the trumpet sounded and Jesus comes to gather up his church. Now what we are about to endeavor into is to be considered hypothetical situation, a "what if" type of look into what might happen in the near future. Now by no means do I call myself a prophet, I am just a servant of the Lord no more than that. You can consider me just a vessel of God. If we go to the book of Revelation in the 17th chapter, you will notice that it repeats itself in the beginning of the chapter it almost seems like you're reading the beginning and end of the 18th chapter all over again. Now I need you to understand that though the book of Revelation was written in Greek; a Hebraic scholar named John, whom is the same one that was a disciple of Jesus, wrote it. I want you to also know that Hebrew is read from right to left, the total opposite from the way we read a book in English. What I mean by this is if you were to go read a book in Hebrew, you would start from the back to the front. Now do you see what I mean about chapters 17th and 18th. Lets go to the first verse so you can see what I'm talking about

(Rev 17:1)

17:1 One of the seven angels who had the seven bowls came and said to me, "Come, I will show you the punishment of the great prostitute, who sits on many waters.

Amazing isn't it? In the (NIV), chapter 18; it says in the 2nd verse that Babylon the Great; she has become a home for demons. The verse says the word <u>she.</u> In the third verse of chapter 18; says she committed adultery with her. It definitely uses the word her and punishment was, handed to her then the verse says who sits on many waters. If you look from an aerial view of New York, it appears to sit on many waters, but remember that Washington got hit as well or could it mean the United States in a whole. You know that the United States sits on many waters. The second verse of chapter 17 startled me because it is almost identical to the third verse in the chapter 18 let us look at them both.

(Rev 17:2)

2 "With her the kings of the earth committed adultery and the inhabitants of the earth were intoxicated with the wine of her adulteries."

(Rev 18:3)

3 "For all the nations have drunk the maddening wine of her adulteries. The kings of the earth committed adultery with her, and the merchants of the earth grew rich from her excessive luxuries."

It looks like if you are reading a book chapter 17 would probably go behind chapter 18 not vice versa. However, as I said, Hebraic scholar wrote this, the next verses become very interesting.

(Rev 17:3-5)

"3 Then the angel carried me away in the Spirit into a desert. There I saw a woman sitting on a scarlet beast that was covered with blasphemous names and had seven heads and ten horns. 4 The woman was dressed in purple and scarlet, and was glittering with gold, precious stones and pearls. She held a golden cup in her hand, filled with abominable things and the filth of

her adulteries. 5 This title was written on her forehead: MYSTERY BABYLON THE GREAT THE MOTHER OF PROSTITUTES AND OF THE ABOMINATIONS OF THE EARTH."

I will not go into detail about this part because I' am not allowed to but I will go in some areas that I can expound on it right now. For the first time in U S history, we had serious woman candidate for the position of United States President. Now lets take a look at what this says, I saw a woman sitting on a scarlet beast, the color scarlet could be considered to be red. Scarlet was the color of blood that is what a typical dictionary tells us and red is one of the colors on our flag. In addition, the emblem of the United States is eagles. Guess what the book of revelation tells us about an eagle? (Rev 12:14) *"The woman was given the two wings of a great eagle, so that she might fly to the place prepared for her in the desert."* This seems to be what would happen if we had a woman become President. Also, let's look at how she is dressed in purple and scarlet. The color purple is considered the color of royalty in the bible. Purple was the color of royal robes in (Judg 8:26), as well as the garments of the wealthy stated in Nelson's Illustrated Bible

Dictionary. The fifth verse tells us that a title is given to her; I believe it is the title of President of the United States. Now if you look at the Queen of England; she has a scepter of gold, with precious stones and pearls on it. Her scepter alone is worth over a million dollars and she wears a crown upon her head as well. So a woman coming into power would not be far-fetched now would it? Also if she is the first woman President, to have a crown or title put upon her head is not far fetched as well because history would be made. As I told you in the beginning of this chapter, we are looking at this from a "what if prospective." I did not exclaim to you to know the future events. However, it seems like the, "what if" might happen in an uncertain future. Now like I said, I cannot go in deep detail about a lot of this as of yet. But we will get in to a little bit to put your Theology to the test. I will tell you this, you cannot put God in a box because He will make a fool of you every time. Now let's go in a little deeper. Some of this is unrevealed mystery hidden for a certain time, not to be released until things happen. Revelation 17:9 tells us this calls for a mind with wisdom, so that leaves me out because I'm as dumb as a box of rocks. I only relay messages

I get from the Father nothing more. Go to the tenth verse and there we will dig in and see what John is revealing to us. (Rev 17:10) *"They are also seven kings. Five have fallen, one is, the other has not yet come; but when he does come, he must remain for a little while."* The six kings John is talking about are powerful empires: Egypt, Assyria, Babylon, Meds-Persia, Greece and Rome, the Roman Empire which was the one existing in John's days. Now the verse says one has not come as of yet, but when it comes, it will remain for just a little while. The United States as a super power has not been known but only a little while. Remember in 1776, our Declaration of Independence was established and by no means, we were called a super power back then. It has been only from the late seventies that we have even been considered as a super power in the world. So just a little over 40 years we have been known as this super power; a force to be reckon with. Some will think that 40 years for an empire is a long span, but the Roman Empire period of domination was from 146B.C to 476 A-D; that's about 622 years. The seventh king that John maybe talking about here is the United States but revelation tells us that there will be an eighth king as well. (Rev 17:11) *"The beast who once was, and now is not, is an eighth king. He belongs to the seven and is going to his destruction."* I found this verse very interesting because it tells us that the eighth king belongs to the seventh and if we are the seventh king we are in the last times. However, do not worry the fourteenth verse tells us they make war against the lamb but the lamb overcomes them lets go there.

(Rev 17:14) *"They will make war against the Lamb, but the Lamb will overcome them because he is Lord of lords and King of kings-and with him will be his called, chosen and faithful followers."*

Now here comes the interesting part. The next verse tell us something important.

(Rev 17:15) *"Then the angel said to me, "The waters you saw, where the prostitute sits, are peoples, multitudes, nations and languages."* Do you know another country that has a multitude of nations and languages then the United States? If so I would like you to tell me where. The verse also says, sitting on many different waters as well. There is no place in the world like the United States that has such riches and is as multicultural as the United States. We are a melting pot of different nationalities. The next two verses are shocking because God himself gives power to the beast to fulfill his purpose. (Rev 17:16-17) *"16 The beast and the ten horns you saw will hate the prostitute. They will bring her to ruin and leave her naked; they will eat her flesh and burn her with fire. 17 For God has put it into their hearts to accomplish his purpose by agreeing to give the beast their power to rule, until God's words are fulfilled."* The verse says they will leave her naked. The word naked could mean different things. The word naked is used in the Bible to express the ideas of poverty (Matt 25:36-44), desolation (Gen 42:9), openness (Heb 4:13), or moral bankruptcy (Rev 3:17) as expounded in a Nelson's Illustrated Bible Dictionary. But the verse also tells us she will be burned with fire as well. The same thing that happened in the 18th chapter. The scariest part is that God gave them the power to do it, to bring His words into fulfillment. *For God has put it into their hearts to accomplish his purpose by agreeing to give the beast their power.* Remember the verse says it is God's purpose, so if you think the devil has power, the verse tells you where He got it. The last verse said to America~ wakeup, pray, repent, and be ye converted. (Rev 17:18) *"The woman you saw is the great city that rules over the kings of the earth."* The great city that rules over the kings of the earth could possibly be our capitol; Washington D.C; if not what other city ever rule kings like our capitol? In addition, in the book of Revelation tells us a woman was given two wings of an eagle. (Rev 12:14) *"The woman was given the two wings of a great eagle, so that she might fly to the place prepared for her in the desert."* What is the United States emblem? It's an eagle! I find that pretty interesting because we are mirror reflection of the Roman Empire. What I mean by that is simply this, the Roman Empire had one head called Caesar, and America has one head called President. The Roman Empire was ran by senators and senators run America. The Roman Empire senators meet in a place called Capitol Leda which means Capitol Hill, our senators meet in Capitol Hill, the emblem of the Roman Empire was an eagle, and our emblem is an eagle. The Roman Empire fell because of greed and a homosexual spirit that entered them, men were allowed to fondle little boys, and statues of such acts were open for public display. Because of the greed of the Roman Empire, high taxation caused every citizen of Rome to lose their land and home to the government. Does that sound familiar? History always has a way of repeating itself. That is what the Bible tells us. (Eccl 1:9-10)*"What has been will be again, what has been done will be done again; there is nothing new under the sun. Is there anything of which one can say, "Look! This is something new"? It was here already, long ago; it was here before our time."* I bring this verse in the conclusions to let you know the Roman Empire fell and if we are following, their example, America will fall as well. Now is the time for us to realize the time we're living in, now is the time for crying out to God for mercy. The Bible says He will hear if we humble ourselves.

(2 Chron 7:14)*"if my people, who are called by my name, will humble themselves and pray and seek my face and turn from their wicked ways, then will I hear from heaven and will forgive their sin and will heal their land."*

CHAPTER 5

A Time to Repent

The word repent, means in Hebrew to agree and in the Greek to change your mind. Nevertheless, not to many times you will hear preaching on conversion. The word <u>convert</u> means to turn, not to do a 360 degree but a 180 degree turn, because if you do a 360 your start right where you left off and that's in sin. True conversion happens at the point of true acknowledgement of God's love for you, it does not matter what you have done or where you have been in life. God loves you- you're His child. Some are afraid to come to God because they have think they have done too much in life and the devil leads them to believe they have gone too far in sin to turn around. I want you to know that is a lie from the pit of hell! We will find out in this chapter that is not so, that your heavenly Father is waiting patiently for you with open arms. Therefore, we have to disregard what the world and the devil tell us. Here is the world's philosophy and my rebuttal to their words to the truth of the matter. The Bible has existed for over 3000 years and has never been proven false or in inaccurate by any archaeologist finding. Nor has any scientific dissolution or declaration ever solidified a proper defense to diminish its existence. Psychiatrists would never try to explain the process of conversion. They will not try to analytically explain it, or touch it with logic. They would not try intellectually, or scientifically try to define it. It even eludes them with no hypothesis on this matter. As a matter of fact they try to stay away from the explanation of any supernatural occurrences all together; they call it a phenomenon. They have no scientific or medical conclusion or solution to the matter. But it is amazing to me that this one book has stomped the wise men of the world and the promises of the Lord in it still to this day are still as good as the day that they were written. It is amazing to me that people actually listen to advice of men who do not even believe in the book they cannot prove wrong. Man's philosophy to a person chest high in sin is that they in too deep to get out but let's see what the word of God says about that come let's go there. (Jer 31:3)

"The LORD appeared to us in the past, saying: "I have loved you with an everlasting love; I have drawn you with loving-kindness."

See, the characteristic of the Lord is everlasting love; He changes the mind of a sinner to repent by loving-kindness not wrath. It is the goodness and love of our Lord that causes a person to turn from their wicked ways. *(Rom 2:4)* "Or despisest thou the riches of his goodness and forbearance and longsuffering; not knowing that the goodness of God leadeth thee to repentance?"

Let us look at a story in the Bible of a sinful woman that heard Jesus was in town and when she heard about Him, she came to weep at His feet. (Luke 7:36-43)*" Now one of the Pharisees invited Jesus to have dinner with him, so he went to the Pharisee's house and reclined at the table. When a woman who had lived a sinful life in that town learned that Jesus was eating at the Pharisee's house, she brought an alabaster jar of perfume, and as she stood behind him at his feet weeping, she began to wet his feet with her tears. Then she wiped them with her hair, kissed them and poured perfume on them. When the Pharisee who had invited him saw this, he said to himself, "If this man were a prophet, he would know who is touching him and what kind of woman she is-that she is a sinner."* As the story goes on Jesus turned to Simon, *I have something to tell you." "Tell me, teacher," he said. "Two men owed money to a certain moneylender. One owed him five hundred denarii, and the other fifty. Neither of them had the money to pay him back, so he canceled the debts of both. Now which of them will love him more?"*

Simon replied, "I suppose the one who had the bigger debt canceled."

"You have judged correctly," Jesus said." Now it's amazing to me that Simon did not pickup on Jesus knowing his very thoughts because the scripture says he said that to himself. However, if you notice Jesus said the one who owed the bigger debt would love his master more than the one that thought he was morally correct because his sins were less than the other. Jesus also says in verse 47," Therefore, I tell you, her many sins have been forgiven-for she loved much. But he who has been forgiven little loves little." See, the person that thinks they lived a moral life, that he or she has done no wrong, are in more danger than the one that is embellished, as an everyday sinner. Because no one has to tell a sinner they are sinning they

already know that, try to tell them something productive like how to stop sinning. It's the love of God that causes men to stop sinning. The book of Romans 3:23 tells us that all have sinned and fallen short of the glory of God it was the Lords grace and mercy that saved us not our human morality. Some people think because they live a so call moral life they need not to repent because they have done nothing wrong in their own eyes. However, the word of God tells me everything that is not done in faith in him is sin. (Rom 14:23) *"And everything that does not come from faith is sin."* Christ died on a cross to set you and me free from the yoke of sin, but understand what I mean by this if you look at it from a heavenly perspective not an earthly. The Bible tells us when Adam and Eve were placed in the garden, and all they were responsible for was tending and keeping the garden, they did not have the burdens of life on them. Christ before going to Calvary was in a garden called Gethsemane, the olive press that is what it means. In the first Garden of Eden, God cursed the ground but in the garden of Gethsemane, the curse was redeemed, by Jesus blood falling upon the ground because the gospel of Luke says. (Luke 22:44) *"And being in anguish, he prayed more earnestly, and his sweat was like drops of blood falling to the ground."* The first place where Christ bleeds was in the garden on the ground, releasing us from the curse from the beginning. So how does this apply to us? When Christ died on the cross He fulfilled a promise for forgiveness of sins, not some sin but all sins, that of the whole world. Your past, future and present sins were and are forgiven on that cross. He releases a way to heaven this way in which is to believe in the one who died for you, Jesus.

(Rom 3:24-28) *"being justified freely by His grace through the redemption that is in Christ Jesus, whom God set forth as a propitiation by His blood, through faith, to demonstrate His righteousness, because in His forbearance God had passed over the sins that were previously committed, to demonstrate at the present time His righteousness, that He might be just and the justifier of the one who has faith in Jesus.*

Where is boasting then? It is excluded. By what law? Of works? No, but by the law of faith. Therefore we conclude that a man is justified by faith apart from the deeds of the law."

So, if you think you moral actions have kept you in the grace of Gods presence; think again. The book of James states if you stumble on one point of the law you have failed it all.

(James 2:9-11)

"But if you show favoritism, you sin and are convicted by the law as lawbreakers. For whoever keeps the whole law and yet stumbles at just one point is guilty of breaking all of it. For he who said, "Do not commit adultery," also said, "Do not murder." If you do not commit adultery but do commit murder, you have become a lawbreaker." Sometimes we as being humans like to think we are not, that bad of a person. We are not like a murderer or a sex-offender but really, the truth of the matter is, sin is sin to God that is the whole reason he had to send His son. Picture it this way, all Adam had to do is not eat of the tree that God told him not to eat of and all you have to do is believe what He did on the cross was real. That you're forgiven for all sins

done in the present, past and future. You are forgiven; but do you believe you're forgiven? This is the point I'm trying to make! When you really believe in Jesus Christ as your Lord and Savior; the Holy Spirit grafts you into His family, you become a new man, so the old man dies and the new man lives like a new creation. That newborn creation is like a newborn baby to the world. The baby does not come out of their mother's womb and is reminded of all the failure in its life, not because the baby in its own mind has never failed, he is new. When you accept Christ in your life you undergo the same process, its like you never sinned before, you are as white as snow. Why? because God does not look at you or your sin now, He looks at the perfect sacrifice of an unblemished lamb which is Jesus. Back in the days of Moses, they had a high priest sacrifice an unblemished lamb for the sins of the people and his own sins as well. So the priest was never examined by God, the lamb being sacrifice was examined by God, the lamb had to be without blemish, not the high priest. It clearly states that in the book of Hebrews why, because the priest had sinned as well as the people. (Heb 9:6-7) "*When everything had been arranged like this, the priests entered regularly into the outer room to carry on their ministry. But only the high priest entered the inner room, and that only once a year, and never without blood, which he offered for himself and for the sins the people had committed in ignorance."* Now just picture this for a second, the scripture says here that the high priest himself offered for himself a sin offering. This is a person in a position that you would think he, as a high priest would have no sin in his life to make an offering. Therefore, I guess even a high priest having sin in his life and his responsibility in life was to know what and how to please God. Moreover, the Lord entrusting him with the Torah and the Laws of God Almighty knowing what sin was and how it displeases the Lord; he still sinned. So when somebody tells me they can live life without sinning, I say back to them no you cannot, see you been trying to live morally and you fail daily. The law was given to us to show us we can't live by it, let me prove my point to you in the book of (Gal 3:22-25) *"But the Scripture declares that the whole world is a prisoner of sin, so that what was promised, being given through faith in Jesus Christ, might be given to those who believe. Before this faith came, we were held prisoners by the law, locked up until faith should be revealed. So the law was put in charge to lead us to Christ that we might be justified by faith. Now that faith has come, we are no longer under the supervision of the law."* The word says that the law was put in charge to lead us to Christ. Therefore, what does it mean, the law was based on by human efforts, meaning living according to the law and by the commandments. Nevertheless, no one could keep them, not even the high priest. There was a certain rich man that came to Jesus and he asked Master what must I do to obtain eternal life. (Mark 10:17-22)*"Now as He was going out on the road, one came running, knelt before Him, and asked Him, "Good Teacher, what shall I do that I may inherit eternal life?" So Jesus said to him, "Why do you call Me good? No one is good but One, that is, God. You know the commandments: 'Do not commit adultery,' 'Do not murder,' 'Do not steal,' 'Do not bear false witness,' 'Do not defraud,' 'Honor your father and your mother.' " And he answered and said to Him, "Teacher, all these I have observed from my youth." Then Jesus, looking at him, loved him, and said to him, "One thing you lack: Go your way, sell whatever you have and give to the poor, and you will have treasure in heaven; and come, take up the cross, and follow Me."* The young man asked Jesus what must he do to inherit eternal life and Jesus referred him to the commandments, not the law. Which is to Love your Lord, your God with all your heart, soul and mind and to love your neighbor as yourself. These are the only two commandments of the New Testament. If you look at the first four commandments, you will keep if you love God and the last six you will keep if you loved your neighbor. But the young man's reply back was, I have observed them meaning he kept them; but Jesus said there's one thing you still lack which was love, so he was coming up short of the mark. Remember the book of James says that if you break one point of the law, you broke it all. We are commanded to love, but it is the love of a Holy God that has kept us, not our love for him. In His love for us; He sent his very best Jesus His only Son. So remember that once you really repent and accept Jesus as your Lord and Savior; you are engrafted into the family of God. Your righteousness does not count on personal achievements, what you do right, and what do wrong, it is based on how you believe. Do you believe that He loves you and that there is nothing on earth to separate you from His love? It's all about love, the only two commandments in New Testament is love. The bible tells us that love covers all sin. See, it was His love on a cross that paid in full for what we had lost, which is our destiny in him. Now that the sacrifice is complete, the penalty of sin was paid in full. This is why the last thing He said was "It Is Finished". Meaning no more sacrifice has to be made for you, all you have to do is believe in Him, believe He loves you, and receive the love He has for you. Yes, you might say you do not deserve it; no one does! God did it because He created you so you're his child. He loves you with a love no one could even comprehend. Before He created the earth or created anything, He left an inheritance for you. (Matt 25:34-35)***"Then the King will say to those on His right hand, 'Come, you blessed of My Father, inherit the kingdom prepared for you from the foundation of the world:"*** He did all that you see, just for you, that's how much He loves you. This is the point I am trying to make. There is not one person on the face of this planet that does not seek love. Maybe life has hit you so hard that you think no one could ever love you and you have given up on it. However, deep down inside you still desire it. Why? Because God created you for love. That's why I don't care if you think a serial killer, antisocial, stuck on themselves individual or someone that plays around with one woman to the next (a player) don't want love; they do actually, that is why they're acting the way they are. They got hurt deeply by someone; and they think they can find happiness in misery. A person that has been hurt finds pleasure in others suffering but really on the inside they even become more depressed and miserable. Because of insecurity, they like to see another person fail because the devil has made them think to themselves I am a failure and they don't want anyone else to succeed. Why, because if no one else fails, they would be all alone not knowing the devil has them there already. No one wants to live without knowing someone loves them. Sometimes you will see people angry or hostile in their personality. People like that are dysfunctional socially; they stay away from people and do not like to engage in too much conversation. This is called building a wall of protection because they were hurt. Therefore, they will not let anyone get close to them because someone they love hurt them so bad that it left a scar. They are wounded because they try not have feelings for people or get emotionally connected to someone they can protect themselves. This is the devil defense, as I like to call it, he tells you no one really cares about you and you believe him so you start going through life feeling empty. You feel empty because you lack love, the very substance you were designed to be filled with. The bible says we are earthen vessels, a vessel is designed to carry things. It is not created to be empty; (2 Cor 4:7) *"But we have this treasure in earthen vessels, so that the surpassing greatness of the power will be of God and not from ourselves."* See, the bible calls us earthen vessels and we are designed to hold a substance, scripture tells us it is treasure and that treasure is God's unfailing love for us. The bible says He loved us first; it is His love for us that calls us until our dying day saying come my child you are loved. (Eph 3:16-19)*"I pray that out of his glorious riches he may strengthen you with power through his Spirit in your inner being, so that Christ may dwell in your hearts through faith. And I pray that you, being rooted and established in love, may have power, together with all the saints, to grasp how wide and long and high and deep is the love of Christ, and to know this love that surpasses knowledge-that you may be filled to the measure of all the fullness of God."* Understand this today that nothing can separate us from His love; no matter how far you run or what bad circumstance you cause yourself to be in. Nothing can cause the Lord to stop loving you. It tells us that in the book of Romans 8:35-39 Paul begins to ask us, who shall separate us from the love of God and nothing and no one shall separate us from the love of Christ. If you believe this today and know that you have been lead a stray by the worlds way; please understand this, all you have to do is ask love to come into your heart and believe that Jesus died for you. The bible tells us that if we knock, the door shall be opened. If we seek we shall find Him, all you have to do is to change your mind and think a new way. The book of Acts tells us Paul was on the way to Damascus when he saw a light and then a voice said from Heaven say "Paul why do you persecute me?" (Acts9: 3-6) Paul's thinking was wrong, he believed that he was doing the work of the Lord but he found out he was actually fighting against God. The Bible says that a light shined around him and tells us that when God came to Moses, He also came in the form of a light a burning bush. The Bible tells us in (Genesis 1:3) the first thing God put upon the earth was light to separate light from darkness, that light was Jesus. I say this because in (John 1:4-5). It says this, *"In him was life, and that life was the light of men. The light shines in the darkness, but the darkness has not understood it."*

Well the reason most people want to stay in darkness is because light exposes their flaws, and if they come to the light, all their flaws will be exposed. However, they really do not understand that Christ died on the cross to make them flawless in the midst of their light meaning in the presence of their Creator. The knowledge of knowing Christ made you perfect at the cross and will enable them to be flawless in the sight of God. There is a reflection on this; remember in the book of Hebrews the high priest was never examined for sin it was the lamb that had to be flawless and without blemish. Well, one of the names of Christ is the Lamb of God that took upon Himself the sins of the world. So if you think God examined your sins after you repent them to Him, remember this, God is not examining you. He is looking at the perfect work of the cross, Jesus the unblemished lamb. If you want to see a pure picture of grace look at this. God used two murderers, one He entrusted the law, Moses and the other Paul, entrusted with the Grace of our Lord. So if you think you have done too much in your life for God to love you, think again. Remember in the Greek repent means to change your mind. Just change your mind today because the Lord Loves You!

Come let us pray together! Lord please forgive me for I am a sinner. I have sinned against you in word, thought, and deed by what I have done and by what I have left undone. Today, come into my life and into my heart, change me through and through today. I agree that I have done wrong in your sight. And I ask you to forgive me. Please accept me as Your child in Your Kingdom, I agree with Your will for my life and Your plans are pleasing to me. I know You have good plans for my life and You will never leave me nor forsake me. I here now make this decree, I believe in Your Son Jesus, as the only way to your Kingdom in Heaven. I believe He died and rose on the third day. I believe He is King of Kings and Lord of Lords. I believe that His death made atonement for all my sin and by His stripes I am healed delivered and set free from death. In Jesus, name Amen and Amen.

If you just prayed that prayer and meant it in your heart, you are saved and a child of the Most High King Jesus.

CHAPTER 6

Inviting the Holy Spirit to Live Within Your Moral Body

The first thing you have to understand, the Holy Spirit is a person and He will never go anywhere that he is not invited. There are so many different denominations claiming to truly know Him and have Him in their lives; but in reality, they do not. I want to tell you that without miraculous signs and wonders; I doubt they have ever felt the presence of the All Mighty Father and His most precious Spirit. If they have, they would never be the same. Now I would like to explain what I mean by this. My sons Christian and Angel ask me too take them to a movie called the devil inside and ask me can a demon possessed a Catholic priest. My response back to them was yes because a Catholic priest is not spirit filled. That's why it is very easy for a demon to possess them; I will take you to scripture to prove to you what I mean by this statement. (Acts 19:13-16) "Some Jews who went around driving out evil spirits tried to invoke the name of the Lord Jesus over those who were demon-possessed. They would say, "In the name of Jesus, whom Paul preaches, I command you to come out." Seven sons of Sceva, a Jewish chief priest, were doing this. [One day] the evil spirit answered them, "Jesus I know, and I know about Paul, but who are you?" Then the man who had the evil spirit jumped on them and overpowered them all. He gave them such a beating that they ran out of the house naked and bleeding." You have to be spirit filled to tell a demon where to go. They will know if you have the authority to do so or not. As you can see, the evil spirit beat the priest and their clothes were taken off of them. So that tell us that demon had no respect for their authority. You have to have a personal relationship with Jesus and have His most precious Holy Spirit in you. So how do we get Him to dwell in us? We just have to ask with a sincere heart and you have to be real with Him. The bible says knock and the door will be answered, ask and it will be given to you, seek and yea shall find (Matt7:7-8). Now I want you to know there are some things in your life you will have to depart from. Things such as unbelief, and a desire to sin but that is the price you have to pay, for Him to come in with all power. All you have to do is believe in Him with all your heart and lean not on your own understanding. Remember when Jesus sends his disciples out; He gave them power and authority over every form of sickness, diseases and demonic forces. (Luke 9:1-2) "When Jesus had called the Twelve together, He gave them power and authority to drive out all demons and to cure diseases, and He sent them out to preach the kingdom of God and to heal the sick." This scripture clearly tell us, He gave them all power and authority to drive out all demons not just some. So why would you want to go in a place holding a crucifix in your hand thinking that is going to scare a demon? It is the one who died on the crucifix and His name is Jesus that scares the demons. The only thing I use to tell the devil and his demons where to go is I rebuke you and the name of Jesus. There and only there, is where the power is that He vested unto us. You holding a cross in your hand means nothing because it is the one who died on the cross. I once visited a Catholic church that was in need to repair their air-condition unit. This sweet nun gave me some Mary water to cast out devils and demons. I started to laugh to myself and then I became very sad because those people have no clue how to even defend themselves. I hope you do not believe you can cast a demon out in

Mary's name because that is a lie from the pit of hell. There is nowhere in your bible where it tells you such a hypocrisy, that is complete ludicrous. It is only in the name of Jesus that a person is healed, delivered, save and have authority and power over the devil. You can pray to Mary all day long and nothing is going to happen at all. This is a complete lie from the devil. The reason he shows you such foolishness is because if he told you the truth; he would be destroying himself. What name does the bible tells us to use? Let us go there! (Mark 16:16-18) "Whoever believes and is baptized will be saved, but whoever does not believe will be condemned. And these signs will accompany those who believe: In my name they will drive out demons; they will speak in new tongues; they will pick up snakes with their hands; and when they drink deadly poison, it will not hurt them at all; they will place their hands on sick people, and they will get well." Who is the one talking to His disciples? Jesus! and it is clearly in my name meaning His name; they will drive out demons not in Mary's name. In addition, this scripture gives you a clear understanding how to be baptized in the Holy Spirit. It is a little word called "believe in" what and "believe in" who. In Jesus name and believe that He is the Son of God, He died for your sins, and He rose from the dead. Moreover, all power and authority has been given to Him by the Father, He and only He alone is our source of strength. So I will tell you this, seek yea first the kingdom of God and all things will be added unto you. There is nothing on planet earth that exists without Him creating it, all things were created by Him and for Him. (Col 1:16-17) "For by him all things were created: things in heaven and on earth, visible and invisible, whether thrones or powers or rulers or authorities; all things were created by him and for him. He is before all things, and in him all things hold together." I just got back from preaching in Haiti and as they took me to one of their villages in the mountain, I saw a beautiful waterfall. Bishop Jean Willmer told me they gave that place to the devil worshipers. As I was standing there, I notice a young lady dress in all red teaching witch craft. When she saw me, she went in hiding around the rocks because she was afraid to do witch craft around servants of the Lord. If they gave them this place and we were supposed to be the visitors, they should've had no problem demonstrating their black magic power! They knew who had the real power, it is in the most precious name of Jesus.

So believe me, He knows how to defeat the devil because it already has been done for us- it happen on a cross on Calvary when He said it is finished! Now Jesus told His disciples when the Holy Spirit comes upon you, you shall receive power (Acts 1:8) He also told them they would speak in new tongues as the Spirit enabled them. (Acts 2:4) Now many of Pentecostal pastors or churches will tell you if you cannot speak in tongues, you are not spirit filled. This is a misconception. You cannot put a limit on God and say He only works this one way. Let's take a man named Smith Wigglesworth for instance. Brother Wigglesworth says he was baptized in the Holy Spirit and three months later, he began to speak in an unknown tongue. I'm going to believe a man that has been known by the anointing of the Holy Spirit to raise 14 people from the dead and healed hundreds of thousands of people from cancer, sugar diabetes, you name it the Holy Spirit in him did it more so than a religious preacher or church which cannot pray a cough off an infant or tell a demon where to go. All you have to do to receive the Holy Spirit is just ask with a sincere heart that's all. Ask Him to come in and say "Lord have your way, I surrender all to you". When you do; His precious Holy Spirit will come in and change you, trust me when I tell you this, your never going to be the same when this happens. Now when this take place know that He is with you and there is no demon in earth or hell that can stop you. You will also have to know there are different levels of anointing. There is a process you will have to endure to receive a higher anointing from the Lord. He will not just give all power to those that are still babes. However, know there is no demon that can possess you if you are spirit filled. That is a powerful assurance. Even though you might not have the power to tell a demon to come off another person; you will have the power to make him flee from you in the name of Jesus and he will have to leave. It is in the power of the most precious name of Jesus and the power of his blood that demons have to flee. However, if we think we are superior to all the other denominations because we are Spirit filled and they are not, we are in era. They are our brothers and sister of the same faith. We have to show them the truth in love and not in hatred. With a sincere heart and not boasting, making them feel they are inferior to us. Remember Jesus never look down on His disciples. He corrected them in love. It tells us in the book of 1Peter to honor our brothers and sisters. (1 Peter 2:17-18) "Honor all people. Love the brotherhood. Fear God. Honor the king. Servants, be submissive to your masters with all fear, not only to the good and gentle, but also to the harsh." I believe if we can set aside our differences, we can make a difference in the world. It's really hard to be in denial when a demon possessed person becomes sane in front of everyone. When a deaf mute person start hearing and talking, it is really hard to say that the power of God did not heal them. The Holy Spirit can prove Himself to be the healer all by himself, believe me I can do nothing without the Holy Ghost. I have no power at all! It is Him and only Him that does it. So if we look at it in this way and show love to those that have never met the Holy Spirit or never been filled with the spirit, we can actually take the churches and start uniting them. Now I understand that there are some priests and pastors, which will be stricken by the spirit of jealousy; as well as with insecurities, some were never called by the Lord to pastor, and some have their own personal agendas from satan. I know this will cause this movement to have friction. Nevertheless, you have to look at it this way; without friction there can be no movement. The word crisis in Hebrew means "promotion" and without an enemy, you cannot go into your next season. So, do not be afraid to share the gift of the Holy Spirit with those in other denominations and other religions because you might be saving someone's life by doing so. Remember what Jesus said, if you deny me before men, I would deny you before my Father. (Matt 10:32-33) "Whosoever therefore shall confess me before men, him will I confess also before my Father which is in heaven. But whosoever shall deny me before men, him will I also deny before my Father which is in heaven." In closing remember that love covers all sin and those that or around you that are in darkness need the light of love that is in you. So, let your light shine in the mist of darkness and try to remember at one time you were in the same place of hopelessness that they are presently in, therefore, it is your job to introduce them to the light of love Jesus. So let you light shine! This is why I offer my services to any denomination and religion so they can see with their own eyes the power of the Holy Spirit. The Catholic denomination has what you would call priests that perform exorcism. In every

Catholic diocese, I offer my services to them for free and ask them to get me the hardest case they have. Not to show off but so they see with their own eyes the power of the Holy Spirit. There is no demon that can withstand Him once He shows up. Believe me! My offer to my brothers and sister still stand if they need my help, I will be there for them in love. This is the love I want all the people upon the face of the whole earth to experience.

(Titus 3:4-6) "But when the kindness and the love of God our Savior toward man appeared, not by works of righteousness which we have done, but according to His mercy He saved us, through the washing of regeneration and renewing of the Holy Spirit, whom He poured out on us abundantly through Jesus Christ our Savior,." My prayer is simply that all of God magnificent children receive this most wonderful loving power of the Holy Spirit. Pentecostal, Baptist, Lutheran and Methodist all have some strong points and weak points as well as the Catholic. However, a lesson that can be learned is the importance of good stewardship. Where the up keep of their buildings are concerned, buildings that are over two decades old are still in immaculate condition. Therefore, we all can learn some things from one another, which is edifying to the body of our Lord, which is the church and is substantial and beneficial to our ministries.

Understanding the Holy Spirit in the God Head

This part of the chapter will explain who the Holy Spirit is in the God Head. First you have the Father God who is Yahweh meaning He is the creator in the Godhead but we all know the essence of his begin is Love. Then you have Jesus, which is the redeemer in the Godhead. Then you have the Holy Spirit, which is the sanctifier in the Godhead. Therefore, if you understand the characteristics of the Godhead you will not be confused. Here are some of the characteristics of the Holy Spirit the word sanctifier means SANCTIFICATION Grk. hagiasmos, "separation, a setting apart"). The Heb. term qodesh, rendered "sanctify," has a corresponding meaning. The dominant idea of sanctification, therefore, is separation from the secular and sinful and setting apart for a sacred purpose. So he is our sanctifier it tell us that in the book of Romans. (Rom 15:16) "to be a minister of Christ Jesus to the Gentiles with the priestly duty of proclaiming the gospel of God, so that the Gentiles might become an offering acceptable to God, sanctified by the Holy Spirit." He will teach you how too pray and what to pray for He prays for you and intercedes for us as well it tell us that in (Rom 8:26-27). So when you get up in the morning and don't know what to pray for just ask he to help you pray and he will teach you. Speak to him just as if you would a person because he is a person. Remember the bible tell us we can grieved the Holy Spirit he is a person, because only people can feel the feeling of being grieved. (Eph 4:30-32) the book of (Isa 63:10) "Yet they rebelled and grieved his Holy Spirit." They rebelled mean they were disobedience Gods commandment cause the Holy Spirit to be grieved and it is the same with us when we disobey God. The word of God says obedience means more than sacrifice. The Holy Spirit is the counselor that Jesus told the disciples would come. (John 14:26) "But the Counselor, the Holy Spirit, whom the Father will send in my name, will teach you all things and will remind you of everything I have said to you." He is the power of God almighty he performs every miraculous sign and wonder and every healing. (Acts 1:8) "But you will receive power when the Holy Spirit comes on you; and you will be my witnesses in Jerusalem, and in all Judea and Samaria, and to the ends of the earth." (Acts 10:38) "How God anointed Jesus of Nazareth with the Holy Spirit and power, and how he went around doing good and healing all who were under the power of the devil, because God was with him." Some theologians mighty argue this point and say not healings but I will take them to a place in the book of Mark where a woman was there who had been subject to bleeding for twelve years. The bible tells us that she touched his garment and she was healed. It also tell that Jesus himself said someone touch me because power has left me. (Mark 5:30)"At once Jesus realized that power had gone out from him. He turned around in the crowd and asked, "Who touched my clothes?" What power was Jesus talking about, it was Holy Ghost power that was vested to him after he went for testing in the desert before than the book of Luke say he was full of the spirit but after he past the tested it says he came back in the power of the spirit (Luke 4:1-14). Which takes us to the next characteristics of the Holy Spirit he also leads us when we don't know where to go he will lead you if you let Him. The bible tell man named Simon was led by the spirit in (Luke 2:27-28)"Moved by the Spirit, he went into the temple courts. When the parents brought in the child Jesus to do for him what the custom of the Law required, Simeon took him in his arms and praised God, saying:" We also know that the bible tell us Jesus himself was led in the deserted by the spirit. The next characteristic of the Holy Spirit is word of wisdom and knowledge of thing hidden. He can reveal heavenly wisdom that earthly wisdom will not be able to comprehend (1Cor. 1:18-19) "For the message of the cross is foolishness to those who are perishing, but to us who are being saved it is the power of God. For it is written: "I will destroy the wisdom of the wise; the intelligence of the intelligent I will frustrate." It is very clear that the Holy Spirit can give you wisdom on matters of earthly principles neither acquired by you or the wisdom of man. He is all knowing because he has a direct access to unlimited resources the Father the creator of all things. So I suggest you get to know Him, all you have to do is just ask Him to help you just say to him, Holy Spirit you are welcome in my body mind and soul. Please come in and He will.

Chapter 7

It's Time to Find Our True Identity

The most amazing thing to me is people can go through their whole life and not know whom they really are. They do not even acknowledge the God who made them, the very one who surrounds them with His love and protection everyday. I understand that sometimes children born in other countries have parents that worship pagan gods and maybe they had parents that never knew the Lord. On the other hand, they could have been abandoned as a child and they do not even know who their own parents are much less who Jesus is. I am not including them because they have a legitimate excuse why they have not ever heard of the gospel or the name of Jesus spoken to them. I am addressing the ones that have heard the gospel preached to them and not sought after the true essence of their purpose in life. Some ask the Holy Spirit to come into them, but because they lack mercy for a brother or sister, they hinder their own relationship. They grieve the Holy Spirit with an unforgiving heart and wonder why He is not pleased with them. It was the forgiveness of an almighty God, which sent His son to die on a cross for us. He forgave us so how can we hold a grudge against another brother. The heart of the Lord is mercy and compassion for his children. Because He knows them and us better than we know ourselves. He knows what type of guidance they had at an adolescent age, if any at all. See, a lot of people have been abandoned as babies and had no one to teach them proper mannerisms or teach them about having a relationship with Jesus so they were neglected at the most significant time of their lives. When it matters the most no one was there for them, they were left for dead so they had to learn survival tactics that suited them for the moment. They were never taught about faith or believing in the unseen God for their needs. They only knew that the very woman that bore them abandoned them and left them for dead. For someone like that it is hard for them to believe that the Lord loves them so much. That He saved them even as a baby when they were rejected by a mother that should have taken care of them and nursed, fed and protected them. The Bible says in (Ezek 16:4-6) *On the day you were born your cord was not cut, nor were you washed with water to make you clean, nor were you rubbed with salt or wrapped in cloths. 5 No one looked on you with pity or had compassion enough to do any of these things for you. Rather, you were thrown out into the open field, for on the day you were born you were despised. 6 "'Then I passed by and saw you kicking about in your blood, and as you lay there in your blood I said to you, "Live!"* The cord not being cut is a sign of baggage, which the child will carry around for the rest of their lives. You see the cord is connected to the placenta and the cord provides nourishment for the child, it brings them life. However, once the placenta is removed from the mother's womb it could cause infection and disease causing death or permanent damage. Therefore, the cord needs to be cut to stop an infection from pursuing the helpless party. However the cord being cut might stop infection and disease from affecting the child but being despised and left for dead they will carry it around with them for the rest of their lives. That is what we can and will call baggage, from not being loved by someone that is suppose too. A life of being rejected at birth is hard to overcome for several reasons, for one you were despised from the beginning and all ready, not all odds are in your favor. Victory is nowhere near on the horizon, odds are stacked against you making it tough just getting your daily necessities met as in food, water, clothes and shelter. Having dreams of having a normal life like, making it to college or just getting through high school or not being looked at as an outcast by society becomes a battle. Alternatively, how about a person that did have parents but were verbally, physically and sexual abuse. That person could very easily slip away and try to reformulate self-worth. A question might form in their mind, as why did they even bring me into this world to abuse and use me. So if you were able to look into someone's childhood as the Lord, you might have a different opinion of that person and have pity and mercy for them. You would even probably start praying that they would turn to the Lord to get the victory that they most desperately need. You see, a person that has an over critical nature or their negative about everything just didn't get up one day and say, I want to be miserable and insecure for the rest of my life. They might act like that did not happen, though, something traumatic happen in their lives that caused this. Just as a dirty area on your body can cause an infection and that infection could cause a disease. On the other hand this is the effect of an unhealthy childhood that caused this root of infection to grow without the hope of being suppressed or even eliminated. A person with an over critical nature is one that always finds joy in putting others down. They are constantly looking for flaws in people to make jokes about them. The traits of this person are gossip, slander and sowing discord. They feel another person's failures are to make them feel better about themselves; it actually causes them joy when someone does worse than them. They feel they have to become the perpetrator instead of becoming the victim. Now you might be asking yourself," why is he speaking about all this if this chapter is about finding your true identity. Some might think because they find themselves with this particular defect in their personality it means this is who they are and that is just not the case at all. Or they choose a certain occupation for their lives and think their occupation must be what God called them for, even though the job they picked out for themselves causes them to be miserable. I have personally met lawyers that hate their job and wish they could quit but say they're in to far too quit. It is the same for a person that thinks they have too many character flaws to be called by God, chosen to do something amazing and unique. When you start working in the Lords purpose for you, you will find joy, peace and provision for your assignment. See it does not matter what you've done in life or that you were an orphan and you don't know who your parents are. Once you accepted Jesus as the Lord of your life, He is your Father and you have a new DNA meaning you are born again so it is like you are a newborn baby with a no past just as a remarkable future. Your kingdom identity is not in your earthly birthright. Many people might think that is the case but it is not true. Your true identity is in heaven, it is who God called you to be on this earth. He has given you a fresh start and a new beginning that is what the bible tell us in. (2 Cor 5:17) *"Therefore, if anyone is in Christ, he is a new creation; the old has gone, the new has come!"* and it tell us in (1 Peter 1:3-4)*" Praise be to the God and Father of our Lord Jesus Christ! In his great mercy he has given us new birth into a living hope through the resurrection of Jesus Christ from the dead, and into an inheritance that can never perish, spoil or fade-kept in heaven for you."* If you go through the bible, some will say King David was born to be a shepherd of sheep, but that is not true. Because the Lord sent a man named Samuel to tell him who He really was, He was called to be the King of Israel. (1Sam1-13). Let's take a man named Gideon for an example, Gideon was called to be a mighty warrior but Gideon himself did not think that way about himself. The scripture says he was hiding from Midian when the Angel of the Lord found Him; he was threshing wheat in a wine press. Not only was he having an identity crisis, but the wheat he was threshing was losing its identity as well meaning this is just an illustration how fear can cause you to do things out of the ordinary. He was threshing wheat in a wine press. Wheat is not supposed to be put in a wine press! Fear can cause us to lose our identity because you lose all sense of rationality and adhere to a false solution that the devil tells you are practical for fixing the problem. Instead of Gideon asking the Lord, what is my purpose, he saw the situation he was in, looked grim and decided to do what he thought was best at that time. This story is in (Judges 6:1-15). If you read the whole story you will understand the Lord had to send an angel to tell him who he really is in the 12th verse. (Judg

6:12*) "When the angel of the LORD appeared to Gideon, he said, "The LORD is with you, mighty warrior."* As you can see, the angel called him mighty warrior because that is what God called him to be. However, Gideon tried to explain his situation and real identity like God made a mistake about him and did not know the problem he was going through. Gideon said "but sir why has all this happened and how can I save Israel out of Midian's hand, I come from the least of all the tribes of Israel and I am the least of my family". Some of us might be having a Gideon moment thinking I am the least of the least, how can God use me. Put this in your mind God always uses the least likely candidate for the insurmountable and most difficult jobs. Try and remember Joseph was the youngest and so was David, Jacob, and Moses. All were the least likely candidates but God does not look on the outward appearance, He looks at the heart. So, do not think because you were despised from birth that means there is no hope for you, as matter of fact that means you have a very important assignment. I say this because the devil always tries to kill the most anointed from birth. Allow me prove that too you. He tried to kill Jesus and Moses as young babies so if you feel like the black sheep of the family, know today that God has a mighty assignment for you life. Having an over critical nature or thinking negative all the time, doses not mean there is not hope for you. God always uses the ones society calls an outcasts. Let's look at some of the greatest men and women of God, and their character flaws:

- ❖ Moses was a murderer.

- ❖ Aaron was an idol maker causing all the people to sin.

- ❖ David was a murderer and committed adultery.

- ❖ Jonah was disobedient and he was a runner.

- ❖ Jacob was a trickster.

- ❖ Paul was a murderer.

- ❖ Peter had a bad temper and was violent he cut a guards ear off.

- ❖ Thomas was a doubter meaning had a problem with believing.

❖ Matthew was a tax collector.

❖ Mary was a prostitute.

You just have to realize who you really are. Just because you act that way does not mean you can't change, that is a lie from the pit of hell. You can change once you find the Love of the Lord Jesus, you will see a dramatic change in your life and Joy will come rushing in like a unstoppable flood. That joy is unspeakable you can't fathom or explain it, you just want to see everyone you come in contact with, to have it in their lives. Let us pray together for this unspeakable joy, say this aloud and believe it in your heart. All you have to do today is ask the Lord to come in and show you.

Say," most precious Jesus you are welcome in my life in every area and your most precious Holy Spirit is welcome to heal any problem areas in my life that need to be addressed this day. I say goodbye to hatred, bitterness, unforgiveness, pains, rejections, for being abandoned and being despised. I ask you for my kingdom assignment and my purpose in life lead me and direct me everyday. Holy Spirit you are welcome to come into my home and every part of my life. No longer will my past separate me from your future for me I believe in new beginning from now on! Thank you Jesus for your precious blood. Amen

Pray this prayer every morning when you get up.

Holy Spirit, teach me what to say and I will say it.

Tell me what to speak and I will speak it.

Tell me what to think and I will think it.

Tell me where to go and I will go there.

Tell me who to touch and I will touch them.

Tell me who to pray for and I will pray for them.

Tell me what you design me to be and I will be it.

If you just prayed that prayer with me and believed it in your heart you are on your way to your real purpose in life.

Chapter 8

Now is the time to worship the Lord with all your heart

The words used in many churches before the pastor addresses his congregation with a sermon are the words, praise and worship. You might hear music and see dancing, all of this we have learned growing up in the churches; we call it praise and worship. Well I want to show you the true meaning of the words worship and praise. The definition of praise from the New Unger's Bible Dictionary "Praise is an expression of approval or admiration, of gratitude and devotion for blessings received. Praise of God is the acknowledging of His perfections, works, and benefits. Praise and thanksgiving are generally considered as synonymous, yet some distinguish them thus: praise properly terminates in God, on account of His natural Excellencies and perfections." Therefore, praise means more than clapping your hands and stomping your feet; it is an act of sincere adoration for God and for all that he has done and all that He can do in our lives. The word worship means a lot more than what is being engaged in service, and how the congregation or the praise team expresses it. Everywhere there was true worship in the word of God, there was always either a miracle or a blessing transferred to his people. Jesus said that we are to worship Him in spirit and in truth. So what is true worship? The word worship means in the New Unger's Bible Dictionary Heb. shaha (to "bow down"), to prostrate oneself before another in order to do him honor and reverence. Worship also means Heb. shachah to have adoration, humility, submission and obedience or to be of service. Everywhere there was worship in the Bible there was a divine transfer. The devil will always try to get you to worship him instead of the Lord. He tempted Jesus in the desert asking Him to worship him and Jesus replied back that it is written to worship the Lord your God and serve Him only. Since the beginning, the devil has been trying to make man worship him. Remember this; if he tried it with Jesus, he will definitely try with you, but if you understand the meaning of worship it means so much more than singing songs to the Lord. Everywhere there was worship there was a divine transfer. Let's go there so you can see it and acknowledge for yourself. Now remember that to bow down means to totally surrender and be in submission to Him as well as obeying Him, these are characteristics of worship. The book of Genesis tells us that Abraham was tested by God in (Gen 22:1-2) it tell us *"Some time later God tested Abraham. He said to him, "Abraham!" "Here I am," he replied. Then God said, "Take your son, your only son, Isaac, whom you love, and go to the region of Moriah. Sacrifice him there as a burnt offering on one of the mountains I will tell you about."* Now remember that Abraham waited for his son Isaac ninety-nine years and when finally getting him, God then told him to go and sacrifice him. God will always give you the desires of your heart, but there will come a time when He will ask you to sacrifice the gift He gave you to see if you love it more than him. That is true worship because if you are not willing to give it back to Him, your love for the possession is more than for the one who gave you the possession, which is God. Therefore, your possession is at a higher priority in your life than the one who gave it to you in the first place, so in other words, you're worshiping your possession instead of your creator who gave you your possession. Which is more important to you? We see that Abraham trusted God with his most priceless possession which is the promise

God gave him. As the story goes on, he goes to the mountain where God wants him to go. It is called Moriah and the word Moriah in Hebrew means the Lord shall provide. As Abraham was traveling with his son and servants; he tell them something that is the secret to getting blessed in your life. He told them to wait there while he and his son go up to worship the Lord. (Gen 22:5) ***"He said to his servants, "Stay here with the donkey while I and the boy go over there. We will worship and then we will come back to you."*** He used the word worship because worship means obedience, adoration, humility, and submission or to be of service. He obeys God and for doing so, Abraham received a blessing and became the Father of many nations (Genesis 22:15-17). Everywhere in the word of God where there was worship, there is a divine transfer so if you want to see a miracle in your life start noticing what you are worshiping. Anything you put as a priority in your life before you speak or spend time with God is called worship. Some work seven days a week and don't have enough time to tell the Lord thank you just a couple hours out of the week. People do not understand it is because of Him you have a job; it is because of Him that you have life! The air you breathe is His. Think of it this way God made you in a way that you do not have to think to breathe; your body does it naturally. Can you just imagine if you had to remind yourself to breathe every second of every day? How much time will we waste then? Anything that takes up most of your day is something I like to call thinking or fantasizing. From the time you get up to the time you go to sleep you are thinking. But now ask yourself what you are thinking about because the very thing that you think about continuously is getting most of your time. Is it your job, problems, finding the right one to marry, is it on the computer or the TV shows you watch. On the other hand, maybe you have an addiction to the phone, facebook, Internet, or games. These we do not call addictions, we call them sources of entertainment. We want to be entertained every second of every hour of everyday. We tell ourselves we deserve it because we work so hard. But where is God in all of this? He is waiting to just get a minute of your time, so you can ask Him what should I do in life to please you Lord. True worship is making Him a priority in your life. Every morning get up and say "good morning Holy Spirit what would you like me to do today." God forbid but let's say you were sick and you knew that Jesus was the only one that could heal you. Trust me when I say this, I believe your focus everyday would be on Him because you would not know how much time you had left and every second of every day would matter. Therefore, you would think only about being healed and finding him to heal you would only matter to you. This is called true worship. In the book of Mark it tells us that there was a blind man named Bartimaeus. The bible says he was sitting by the roadside begging so his attention was on getting a daily necessity met that is how the blind ate every day they begged. However, the bible tells us that when he heard that Jesus was coming by, Bartimaeus stopped begging for his daily necessity and started begging for the only One that could change his daily routine of being a beggar. He wanted to change things in his life. How do I know? He started to worship the right substance, Jesus, the One that could heal Him so he could earn a living for himself. The bible says he shouted at the top of his lungs. (Mark 10:47-48) *"When he heard that it was Jesus of Nazareth, he began to shout, "Jesus, Son of David, have mercy on me!" Many rebuked him and told him to be quiet, but he shouted all the more, "Son of*

David, have mercy on me!" Now remember, worship means adoration and humility. The beggar had to humble himself to the Lord to get his healing, but let us look at what happens. After the healing takes place the bible tells us, He followed Jesus along the road. (Mark 10:52) *"Go," said Jesus, "your faith has healed you." Immediately he received his sight and followed Jesus along the road."* Also, it is very important to acknowledge that the scripture says he followed Jesus. Anything you follow, you worship. The word <u>follow</u> means in *Webster's dictionary; to accept the authority of or give allegiance to. Many Germans followed Hitler and we know that Germans also worshiped Hitler.* On the very night our precious Jesus was being born, the bible tells us there were wise men that sought after Him and when finding the place he was, in a poor run down manger, they came bearing gifts, but these men did something else, they bowed down and worshiped him. Then the scripture showed us a divine revelation; it tell us that after they worshiped him, their treasures were opened to bear gifts unto him. I believe when worshiping him in spirit and in truth our treasures are open and the very purpose that He called you to do will be revealed

(Matt 2:11). The book of Isaiah tells us, He will give us treasures in darkness. I believe that those treasures He gives us are coming to the understanding of who you are in him. I like to give an illustration of this, a man by the name of Albert Einstein was considered, a failure by society and the college he attended kicked him out because they said he was not smart. As Einstein sat on his job passing patents for other people ideas, an idea came to him from the Lord, it was a secret from heaven called the theory of relativity and he became known as one of the most brilliant minds the world has ever known. (Isa 45:3) *"I will give you the treasures of darkness, riches stored in secret places, so that you may know that I am the LORD, the God of Israel, who summons you by name.* All this can come about, through worshipping the Lord, the book of Psalms says to seek the Lord first and He will give you the desires of your heart. There was a man with leprosy that came to Jesus begging him on his knees to heal him, He said Lord if you are willing can you make me clean. Filled with compassion Jesus reaches out his hand, and touched the man and said be clean (Mark 1:40-42). Now, why do you think this healing took place? I believe it was the point of true worship, the scripture tells us he came on his knees begging. When you come to a place where you are broken down to almost nothing, then you have to go to the only one that can fix your problem and His name is Jesus, because you tried everything else and it has not worked. Back then news traveled fast that Jesus was a healer of all sickness and of every disease and when they actually saw Him they knew it might be their only chance for them to be healed. Therefore, they were not afraid to bow down, ask publicly, and worship Him publicly because they knew He was their last hope of being healed. If we do not look at our situation in the same way no matter whatever it is, financial, physical, mental, sickness or disease, if you don't acknowledge the Lord Jesus in worship we will not see the miracle in our life that we so desperately need. Worship means to bow down before the one true living God Jesus and acknowledge Him as Lord over every area of your life with obedience to Him. He and only He can fix it the way it should be fixed, once and for all. If you go to a doctor, a good one always tries to find the root of the problem because the root contains the true source of the problem. Without removing the root, the problem will always exist, you have to attack the root and remove it, once and for all. True worship comes when you put nothing before the Lord; job, spouse, children, relationships, entertainment, money or possessions, He comes first in your life as if He was your most prized possession and nothing comes before Him in your life, and this is what I call True Worship. I will finish with this verse (John 15:7) *"If you remain in me and my words remain in you, ask whatever you wish, and it will be given you."* Whatever you ask for, it will be given to you, if it is a healing in your financial, physical, mental, sickness or disease it shall be done for you, but first you are to remain in him, that means worship Him in spirit and in truth.

CHAPTER 9

The Process to Gain His Glorious Power

I was asked to speak in a Pastor's conference and the Lord told me to show them the process everyone has to go through in order to see the miraculous signs and wonders. They had been praying to see the miracle of God but have not seen them happen as of yet in their ministries. And the Lord told me; say to them they must endure the process in order to receive my power. But everytime they began to enter the beginning stages of the process they would pray and tell the Lord that it is just too painful to bare. So in this chapter I want to show you the process of getting the Lord's power in your life. There is a big difference between praying and believing for myself compared to praying and believing for someone else's healing or miracle. The first step in gaining His magnificent power is the fact that you have to be broken. Being broken is one of the most difficult things you will ever have to endure. This is when you are willing to really have Jesus have His way with you. It's almost like having a surgical procedure done to your body. As you well know, with any surgical procedure that involves cutting of the flesh, you know there is going to be a lot of pain. Jesus himself had to go through this process! He was sitting at a table with His disciples and He took the bread. The first thing that happens to us is Jesus takes us from the lowest pit of darkness and we become His! Then He gave thanks to the Father. He then broke the bread and told them that it represented his body. He was going to be broken for you! In (Isaiah 53:5) it says "**He was crushed for our iniquities**." Jesus spoke to his disciples and told them that He was the *manna* that came down from heaven! Do you know that in the book of (Numbers 11:7), it states that the *manna* was like coriander seed. Coriander seed is white with a red strip in it and it has to be crushed in order to be eaten. Jesus had to die to Himself first emotionally and submit to the will of the Father. In the book of John he prayed, (John 12:27,28) we see Jesus's prayer in the Garden, "Now my heart is troubled, and what shall I say? 'Father, save me from this hour'? No, it was for this very reason I came to this hour. Father, glorify your name!" The word troubled in the Vines Dictionary means emotionally distressed or an affliction or fearful. In the gospel Luke you will see where Jesus had to pray through the fear, (Luke22:42-44) "Father, if you are willing, take this cup from me; yet not my will, but yours be done." An angel from heaven appeared to him and strengthened him. And being in anguish, he prayed more earnestly, and his sweat was like drops of blood falling to the ground." The last verse gives us a detail description of what Jesus was going through. The word *anguish* is used here which gives us a glimpse of what Jesus was about to face before and on the cross for us. He had to die to Himself and submit His will to the Father. Now, if Jesus had to go through this process of dying to one self, why do you think we are going to avoid it? Guess what? We are not! You see being broken deals with our emotions. The Lord has to reach in and pull out all of our past hurts and failures. That means that you have to deal with the people that hurt you! That means you have to let Jesus into the secret closet, where we have hidden all those bad memories so He can clean them out once and for all! It's amazing how we let the devil use this closet against us over and over. The enemy reminds us of the past hurts and the broken relationships we have gone through. Someone you loved dearly died or might have walked out on you. All those bad memories are in that closet and it's time to say goodbye! Let Jesus remove the baggage we have been carrying around with us for too long, we take it with us in new relationships and wherever we go. Jesus wants you! So why not let Him? He can clean out all the bad things once and for all. Being *broken* is the part of the process that begins to build us thick skin for the next step. We will no longer wear our emotions on our sleeve. Our feelings will not be so easily hurt, or be offended by a person that disagrees with us, nor with those that speak slanderous accusations and start rumors about us. You will begin to see clearly the attacks of the enemy and know that it is just a part of the process. There is a Jewish belief that says there are two things you need to get promoted in the Kingdom of God; an enemy and a crisis! Without either of these two you will not get promoted. Jesus had people talking bad about him, but he showed them love instead of hate. He told his diciples they were going to be persecuted for His name's sake. (Matthew 5:10-12) "Blessed are those who are persecuted because of righteousness, for theirs is the kingdom of heaven. Blessed are you when people insult you, persecute you and falsely say all kinds of evil against you because of me. Rejoice and be glad, because great is your reward in heaven, for in the same way they persecuted the prophets who were before you." Now how many people do you know that will actually rejoice when this happens to them? God's ways are higher than our ways and it is not going to be easy when tough times come your way. That's when you need God to help you through those tough times. Ask for His help. You can learn to use praise as a weapon against the enemy when you want to get angry or depressed. I realize that this goes against every normal emotional response that we have. When someone hurts you or attacks your character, a normal human response is to get even and attack them back for what they did. Just look at the way Jesus handled the situation at His trial. Scriptures say that He did not open his mouth. In (Isa 53:7) it says that, "He was oppressed and afflicted, yet he did not open his mouth." Jesus was broken for us! The book of (Hebrews 5:8-9), "Although he was a son, he learned obedience from what he suffered and, once made perfect, he became the source of eternal salvation for all who obey him." The next part of the process is to be tested with fire. If you look at three of the four gospels you will notice that

Matthew, Mark and Luke all agree that Jesus did not perform any miracles before he was tested! The only place where we see Jesus doing the first miracle before He was tested, is in the book of John. Here we see that Jesus was attending a wedding and when the host ran out of wine. Jesus' mother asked him to help. Jesus replied that, "His time had not yet come", (John 2:4) however, He did the miracle anyway changing water into wine. The gospel of Luke tells us that Jesus had to go in the wilderness to be tempted for forty days. Lets see what happened in the book of (Luke 4:1,2). This takes place after the baptism of Jesus by John the Baptist, "Jesus, full of the Holy Spirit, returned from the Jordan and was led by the Spirit in the desert, where for forty days he was tempted by the devil. He ate nothing during those days, and at the end of them he was hungry." Notice that it says Jesus was full of the Holy Spirit. The point I want to make is that being full of the Spirit, but after the 40 days of testing, He came back in the power of the Spirit. (Luke 4:14) "Jesus returned to Galilee in the power of the Spirit, and news about him spread through the whole countryside." You see He went in full of the Spirit, but when he returned after passing the test *The Power of*

Spirit was given to him. The Power of God is what attracts people! If you take a look at scripture, when Jesus returned *in the power of the Spirit,* news spread through the whole countryside about Him. Why? Because the power of God was manifested in Him and people were being healed that's why. Remember that there was no internet, radio, TV or newspapers. The bible says that the news spread through the whole countryside about him. That's amazing isn't it? In (Mark 5:30-31) there is the story of a woman with an issue of blood, this woman pressed through the crowd to touch the hem of Jesus's garment, "At once Jesus realized that power had gone out from him. He turned around in the crowd and asked, "Who touched my clothes?" "You see the people crowding against you," his disciples answered, "and yet you can ask, 'Who touched me?" If you notice the scripture tells us, there was a crowd that was present. Why? Because the power of God was there. (Luke 6:19) "And the people all tried to touch him, because power was coming from him and healing them all." It is clear to see, when people are getting healed there will always be a crowd of people around, you will not have to advertise. Now, as children of the Most High

God we have access to this power! He has not kept this power for Himself, he gave it to us to have as well. (Luke 9:1) "When Jesus had called the Twelve together, he gave them power and authority to drive out all demons and to cure diseases." This power that was given to the disciples is the same power that is given to us! He does not put a limit on it! In fact He told us in His word that we would do greater works than He did. (John 14:12) "I tell you the truth, anyone who has faith in me will do what I have been doing. He will do even greater things than these, because I am going to the Father." The power of what you *believe* is the key to God's power to overcome any problem in your life. If you do not believe the bible is true, then you cannot have faith to overcome your situation and will never have access to the power of God. Step one is to endure being *broken,* that means to willingly let God clean and heal you of your emotional pain. Step two is being tested with the fire of God. When fire is applied it will purify it. If you have already invited Jesus into your life and seriously wanted Him to change your life, then you will be tested on what you *believe.* The book of James tells us how we are to respond to trials when they come our way, (James 1:2-4)

"Consider it pure joy, my brothers, whenever you face trials of many kinds, because you know that the testing of your faith develops perseverance. Perseverance must finish its work so that you may be mature and complete, not lacking anything." Now James tells us to consider it pure joy when bad circumstances happen to us. What?? How can we do that? How many of us can look at problems from that perspective? This is when you begin to understand that your belief and your faith are being tested! There is good news, in God's school you never fail a test, you just get to take it again until you pass it! When you are tested, stand firm on what you believe and don't let the enemy have his way with you. If you begin to praise God in the mist of your trouble, things change in you favor. This might be another way you can look at your time of testing. A locomotive that is powered by steam needs coal to generate power! The greater the heat, the greater the power. The same principle is used for us in order to gain God's power. The greater the pressure the enemy tries to put on us, the greater power Jesus puts in us to overcome any situation. Here is another perspective. Electricity is an amazing invention. The first element you need to have the power of electricity is called a conductor, which is a wire. This wire in relation to you or me is an empty vessel ready to be used by God. The second thing you need is called laten heat, because without heat there cannot be power. Power comes from heat. The third element you need to have electricity is a capcitor, the function of a capcitor is to store power. To a Christian storing power means spending time with our Heavenly Father in fasting, prayer and in studying the word of God. When you do these things you're storing up power. The fourth element that is needed is a resistor, because without resistance power will remain stagnant meaning no movement is going to take place. That's what I call being full of the spirit, gaining power, but having no access to use it. The resistor to us is the devil. Now, where electricity is involved, the greater the resistances which causes greater amounts of power to be given. If the conductor is too small to handle the resistances, the conductor will burn up. That's why houses have burned down due to someone using the wrong conductor with the wrong resistor. So we can thank our Father for knowing the right resistances to put on us. As you can see the greater the resistances, the greater the power. That means you need to be aware of the kind of anointing you ask for, if you don't what to go through the fire. The book (2 Corinthians 4:8-10) tells us. "We are hard pressed on every side, but not crushed; perplexed, but not in despair; persecuted, but not abandoned; struck down, but not destroyed. We always carry around in our body the death of Jesus, so that the life of Jesus may also be revealed in our body." So right now you might be thinking that everything you have been asking God for has not manifested yet. Maybe He is not hearing my prayers. Well you might just be close to the end of your problems. Maybe your promotion is on the way. Just keep pressing towards the mark of the Most High God. Maybe you feel that no one is using you at the moment and you're seeing persecution from the very people you trusted in. There was a young preacher by the name of William Seymour. No one would let him into their church to preach because he spoke with the spirit of tongues. So the Lord told him My power and Glory is going to show up at your house, on Azusa street. That became known as the biggest revival in the history of United States. Preachers still talk about it to this very day. They want to see another wave of God's Glory. Why?

Because the power of God showed up and showed out. Seymour did not have to advertise! People just started to show up. When God's power shows up, people will flock to you. It was not just local people that showed up at the Azusa Street Revival, they came from all over the world to see what was taking place there. This rivial took place in late 1906. They did not have the technology we have now. It took months for mail or news to get to other countries, but people came anyway. Just remember that there is a process that you're going to have to endure if your want to see the power of the Lord. I was asked to preach in another Pastor's conference in the city Bogota, Colombia. We only had three days to preach, because of another speaking engagement back in the States. But in just those three days and nights of preaching what was only for about sixty to seventy pastor's turned into a glorious revival and the building was packed to capacity. Why did that happen? The Power of God was there, healing and deliverance were taking place. We did not advertise, but the people still packed the place out and it was standing room only. I *believe* that we had endured the process and that is why the power and glory fell. Grace and purpose was being preached and our Father was well pleased. Before I left the states to go on this trip, the persecution I had to endure was almost unbearable. There were a few times I thought that there would be no possible way for me to go. But the Lord made a way and I'm glad that I went to see the miracles that happened. I don't care how things may look at the moment but *believing* the Lord and taking Him at his word is all we have to do. I did not have the money to go, but the Lord told me to preparer sermons anyway and I did. My actions said that I *believed* God, so I acted on it. A check came in the mail unexpectedly! There was enough money for the round trip and to leave a love offering as well with the pastor and people. Just remember when all things are falling apart around you, that God's promises are true and you can stand on them and *believe*! Just *believe* what He spoke and it will come to pass. Act like you already have them. Remember that it's all part of the process! First He has to break you in order to make you, then He has to test you with fire in order to shape and mold you for His purpose. After you have gone through the process, He will then give you out to others around you so that you can be a blessing to them. Thank Him for going though the process for us and praise His name! Jesus the name above all names!

Conclusion: There Is Only One Name

Salvation comes only through the name of Jesus! There is only one name in which you can be saved and go to heaven and that is Jesus. In (John 14:6,) Jesus said, "I am the way and the truth and the life. No one comes to the Father except through me." The only way to the Father is through His son, who is Jesus, and through knowing Him as your Lord and Savior, and having a personal relationship with him. First, we must accept Him as the son of the Most High God.

Let us read what it says in (Romans 10:9-10 :) "That if you confess with your mouth, 'Jesus is Lord,' and believe in your heart that God raised him from the dead, you will be saved. For it is with your heart that you believe and are justified, and it is with your mouth that you confess and are saved." It's simple! It is not hard to be saved. You are called to believe the truth, and the only truth that will stand eternally is the Word of God. If you have never prayed before and desire to take the first step in initiating a relationship with God, I ask you to pray this prayer with me:

Father, I am sorry for what I have done and left undone; please forgive me, for sins known and unknown. Father, I accept your son, Jesus Christ as my Lord and Savior, please wash and cleanse me from all acts of unrighteousness. I humbly repent; have mercy on me and forgive me, Father; it is my will to seek your will and purpose for my life and walk in my Kingdom assignment and to take delight by walking in your will and ways. Amen.

Now, if you just prayed this prayer and you believe it in your heart, you are saved and God calls you His friend. Try to remember that the devil is going to try you by telling you that you are not worthy of Him. (Romans 3:23) states, "For all have sinned and fall short of the glory of God." This means that you and I have sinned, but He still forgives us and loves us; he casts our sins into the sea of forgetfulness, never again to be brought up against us. (Hebrews 10:12,17) Tell the Lord, "Holy is Your name Lord, Hallelujah! Praised be your name above all names, for saving me Lord."

May the Lord keep you, and may His face shine upon you always. God bless, and always fight the Good fight of Faith! And Remember JUST BELIEVE!

Promises & Blessings of God

There is no condemnation in Christ. The Holy Spirit will not condemned you He will convict you.

(Rom 8:1-2)

8:1 Therefore, there is now no condemnation for those who are in Christ Jesus, 2 because through Christ Jesus the law of the Spirit of life set me free from the law of sin and death.

(John 3:16-18)

16 "For God so loved the world that he gave his one and only Son, that whoever believes in him shall not perish but have eternal life. 17 For God did not send his Son into the world to condemn the world, but to save the world through him. 18 Whoever believes in him is not condemned, but whoever does not believe stands condemned already because he has not believed in the name of God's one and only Son.

We are forgiven through the blood of Jesus

(Eph 1:6-8)

7 In him we have redemption through his blood, the forgiveness of sins, in accordance with the riches of God's grace 8 that he lavished on us with all wisdom and understanding.

(Col 1:13-14)

13 For he has rescued us from the dominion of darkness and brought us into the kingdom of the Son he loves, 14 in whom we have redemption, the forgiveness of sins.

(Matt 26:27-28)

27 Then he took the cup, gave thanks and offered it to them, saying, "Drink from it, all of you. 28 This is my blood of the covenant, which is poured out for many for the forgiveness of sins.

(Ps 85:2)

2 You have forgiven the iniquity of Your people; You have covered all their sin.

Ps 103:12

12 as far as the east is from the west, so far has he removed our transgressions from us.

1 John 2:12

12 I write to you, dear children, because your sins have been forgiven on account of his name.

1 John 1:8-9

9 If we confess our sins, he is faithful and just and will forgive us our sins and purify us from all unrighteousness.

All blessing and healing of God will be delayed if we do not Forgive as well.

(Matt 6:14-15)

14 For if you forgive men when they sin against you, your heavenly Father will also forgive you. 15 But if you do not forgive men their sins, your Father will not forgive your sins.

(Matt 18:32-35)

32 "Then the master called the servant in. 'You wicked servant,' he said, 'I canceled all that debt of yours because you begged me to. 33 Shouldn't you have had mercy on your fellow servant just as I had on you?' 34 In anger his master turned him over to the jailers to be tortured, until he should pay back all he owed. 35 "This is how my heavenly Father will treat each of you unless you forgive your brother from your heart."

(Mark 11:24-25)

24 Therefore I tell you, whatever you ask for in prayer, believe that you have received it, and it will be yours. 25 And when you stand praying, if you hold anything against anyone, forgive him, so that your Father in heaven may forgive you your sins."

The Lord Will Provide For You at All Times

Phil 4:19-20

19 And my God shall supply all your need according to His riches in glory by Christ Jesus. 20 Now to our God and Father be glory forever and ever. Amen.

Eph. 3:20

20 Now to Him who is able to do exceedingly abundantly above all that we ask or think, according to the power that works in us,

Gen 22:14

14 So Abraham called that place The LORD Will Provide. And to this day it is said, "On the mountain of the LORD it will be provided."

Gen 45:11

11 I will provide for you there, because five years of famine are still to come. Otherwise you and your household and all who belong to you will become destitute. '

He Wants To Make You Prosper

Jer. 29:11-12

11 For I know the plans I have for you," declares the LORD, "plans to prosper you and not to harm you, plans to give you hope and a future.

3 John 2

2 Beloved, I wish above all things that thou mayest prosper and be in health, even as thy soul prospereth.

Deut 28:8-10

8 The LORD will send a blessing on your barns and on everything you put your hand to. The LORD your God will bless you in the land he is giving you.

9 The LORD will establish you as his holy people, as he promised you on oath, if you keep the commands of the LORD your God and walk in his ways. 10 Then all the peoples on earth will see that you are called by the name of the LORD, and they will fear you.

Isa 45:3

3 I will give you the treasures of darkness, riches stored in secret places, so that you may know that I am the LORD, the God of Israel, who summons you by name.

Deut 8:17-18

17 You may say to yourself, "My power and the strength of my hands have produced this wealth for me." 18 But remember the LORD your God, for it is he who gives you the ability to produce wealth, and so confirms his covenant, which he swore to your forefathers, as it is today.

Remember there is nowhere in the Bible that the Lord gives a blessing, without an act of Faith given to Him first.

John 6:9

9 "Here is a boy with five small barley loaves and two small fish, but how far will they go among so many?"

The boy did not have to give the five loaves and two fish but in doing so, He would not have received twelve baskets full of food.

John 6:12-13

12 When they had all had enough to eat, he said to his disciples, "Gather the pieces that are left over. Let nothing be wasted." 13 So they gathered them and filled twelve baskets with the pieces of the five barley loaves left over by those who had eaten.

Mal 3:10

10 Bring the whole tithe into the storehouse, that there may be food in my house. Test me in this," says the LORD Almighty, "and see if I will not throw open the floodgates of heaven and pour out so much blessing that you will not have room enough for it.

The tithe is just about an act of faith and all miracles and blessings start with an act of faith there is not one healing, miracle, or blessing in the bible that start without the act of faith.

Heb 11:1-3

11:1 Now faith is being sure of what we hope for and certain of what we do not see. 2 This is what the ancients were commended for. 3 By faith we understand that the universe was formed at God's command, so that what is seen was not made out of what was visible.

Heb 11:6

6 And without faith it is impossible to please God, because anyone who comes to him must believe that he exists and that he rewards those who earnestly seek him.

See there is a reward to those that believe in Him.Just believe and you shall receive.

Mark 9:23

23 "'If you can'?" said Jesus. "Everything is possible for him who believes."

Mark 16:17-18

17 And these signs will follow those who believe: In My name they will cast out demons; they will speak with new tongues; 18 they will take up serpents; and if they drink anything deadly, it will by no means hurt them; they will lay hands on the sick, and they will recover."

Matt 21:22

22 If you believe, you will receive whatever you ask for in prayer."

Mark 11:24

24 Therefore I tell you, whatever you ask for in prayer, believe that you have received it, and it will be yours.

John 6:29

29 Jesus answered, "The work of God is this: to believe in the one he has sent."

Eph. 1:18-20

18 I pray also that the eyes of your heart may be enlightened in order that you may know the hope to which he has called you, the riches of his glorious inheritance in the saints, 19 and his incomparably great power for us who believe. That power is like the working of his mighty strength, 20 which he exerted in Christ when he raised him from the dead and seated him at his right hand in the heavenly realms,

We or justified by faith in Christ Jesus not by works. It is not based on what you can do it is based what you believe in what He already completed on the cross.

Acts 13:38-40

38 "Therefore, my brothers, I want you to know that through Jesus the forgiveness of sins is proclaimed to you. 39 Through him everyone who believes is justified from everything you could not be justified from by the Law of Moses.

Rom 5:1-2

5:1 Therefore, since we have been justified through faith, we have peace with God through our Lord Jesus Christ, 2 through whom we have gained access by faith into this grace in which we now stand. And we rejoice in the hope of the glory of God.

Rom 8:30-31

30 And those he predestined, he also called; those he called, he also justified; those he justified, he also glorified. 31 What, then, shall we say in response to this? If God is for us, who can be against us?

1 Cor 6:11

11 And that is what some of you were. But you were washed, you were sanctified, you were justified in the name of the Lord Jesus Christ and by the Spirit of our God.

Gal 2:15-16

15 "We who are Jews by birth and not 'Gentile sinners' 16 know that a man is not justified by observing the law, but by faith in Jesus Christ. So we, too, have put our faith in Christ Jesus that we may be justified by faith in Christ and not by observing the law, because by observing the law no one will be justified.

Gal 3:24-25

24 So the law was put in charge to lead us to Christ that we might be justified by faith. 25 Now that faith has come, we are no longer under the supervision of the law.

He Promise Us Peace in All Things.

John 14:27

27 Peace I leave with you; my peace I give you. I do not give to you as the world gives. Do not let your hearts be troubled and do not be afraid.

Phil 4:7

7 And the peace of God, which transcends all understanding, will guard your hearts and your minds in Christ Jesus.

1 Thes. 5:23-24

23 May God himself, the God of peace, sanctify you through and through. May your whole spirit, soul and body be kept blameless at the coming of our Lord Jesus Christ. **24** The one who calls you is faithful and he will do it.

Heb 13:20-21

20 May the God of peace, who through the blood of the eternal covenant brought back from the dead our Lord Jesus, that great Shepherd of the sheep, 21 equip you with everything good for doing his will, and may he work in us what is pleasing to him, through Jesus Christ, to whom be glory for ever and ever. Amen.

Eph 2:14-18

14 For He Himself is our peace, who has made both one, and has broken down the middle wall of separation, 15 having abolished in His flesh the enmity, that is, the law of commandments contained in ordinances, so as to create in Himself one new man from the two, thus making peace, 16 and that He might reconcile them both to God in one body through the cross, thereby

putting to death the enmity. 17 And He came and preached peace to you who were afar off and to those who were near. 18 For through Him we both have access by one Spirit to the Father. (NKJV)

He Has Vested Power unto Us to Protect us From All the Power of the Devil.

Luke 9:1-2

9:1 When Jesus had called the Twelve together, he gave them power and authority to drive out all demons and to cure diseases, 2 and he sent them out to preach the kingdom of God and to heal the sick.

Luke 10:18-19

18 He replied, "I saw Satan fall like lightning from heaven. 19 I have given you authority to trample on snakes and scorpions and to overcome all the power of the enemy; nothing will harm you.

Acts 1:8

8 But you will receive power when the Holy Spirit comes on you; and you will be my witnesses in Jerusalem, and in all Judea and Samaria, and to the ends of the earth."

Acts 10:38

38 how God anointed Jesus of Nazareth with the Holy Spirit and power, and how he went around doing good and healing all who were under the power of the devil, because God was with him.

Acts 26:17-18

17 I will rescue you from your own people and from the Gentiles. I am sending you to them 18 to open their eyes and turn them from darkness to light, and from the power of Satan to God, so that they may receive forgiveness of sins and a place among those who are sanctified by faith in me.'

Rom 15:17-19

17 Therefore I glory in Christ Jesus in my service to God. 18 I will not venture to speak of anything except what Christ has accomplished through me in leading the Gentiles to obey God by what I have said and done- 19 by the power of signs and miracles, through the power of the Spirit. So from Jerusalem all the way around to Illyricum, I have fully proclaimed the gospel of Christ.

Eph 1:17-22

18 I pray also that the eyes of your heart may be enlightened in order that you may know the hope to which he has called you, the riches of his glorious inheritance in the saints, 19 and his incomparably great power for us who believe. That power is like the working of his mighty strength, 20 which he exerted in Christ when he raised him from the dead and seated him at his right hand in the heavenly realms, **21** far above all rule and authority, power and dominion, and every title that can be given, not only in the present age but also in the one to come.

He has given to us, His most precious and powerful Holy Spirit to show us all thing and give unto us heavenly wisdom.

John 14:25-26

25 "All this I have spoken while still with you. **26** But the Counselor, the Holy Spirit, whom the Father will send in my name, will teach you all things and will remind you of everything I have said to you.

1 Cor 1:17-20

17 For Christ did not send me to baptize, but to preach the gospel-not with words of human wisdom, lest the cross of Christ be emptied of its power. **18** For the message of the cross is foolishness to those who are perishing, but to us who are being saved it is *the power of God. 19 For it is written: "I will destroy the wisdom of the wise;*

the intelligence of the intelligent I will frustrate." 20 Where is the wise man? Where is the scholar? Where is the philosopher of this age? Has not God made foolish the wisdom of the world?

Zech 4:6

6 Then he answered and spake unto me, saying, this is the word of the LORD unto Zerubbabel, saying, not by might, nor by power, but by my spirit, saith the LORD of hosts. (KJV)

I love to use this verse because it is clearly not your power nor your might it is only His spirit in essence it tells us, it is not in your strength, but His that performs the miracle. Some Theologians will say this is not the Holy Spirit because God did not give Him to us before the death of Jesus. This is not an argument it is merely an indication of function and how the function of the Holy Spirit work in our bodies.

1 Sam 10:6-7

6 The Spirit of the LORD will come upon you in power, and you will prophesy with them; and you will be changed into a different person. 7 Once these signs are fulfilled, do whatever your hand finds to do, for God is with you. (NIV)

He Is The One Who Comforts Us At All Times

2 Cor 1:3-4

3 Praise be to the God and Father of our Lord Jesus Christ, the Father of compassion and the God of all comfort, 4 who comforts us in all our troubles, so that we can comfort those in any trouble with the comfort we ourselves have received from God.

2 Cor 1:7

7 And our hope for you is firm, because we know that just as you share in our sufferings, so also you share in our comfort.

Isa 66:13

13 As a mother comforts her child, so will I comfort you; and you will be comforted over Jerusalem."

Ps 86:17

17 Give me a sign of your goodness, that my enemies may see it and be put to shame, for you, O LORD, have helped me and comforted me.

Matt 5:4

4 Blessed are those who mourn, for they will be comforted.

He Has Already Healed you and Delivered you. Just Believe it and Receive it.

1 Peter 2:24

24 He himself bore our sins in his body on the tree, so that we might die to sins and live for righteousness; by his wounds you have been healed.

James 5:16

16 Therefore confess your sins to each other and pray for each other so that you may be healed. The prayer of a righteous man is powerful and effective.

Acts 28:8-9

8 His father was sick in bed, suffering from fever and dysentery. Paul went in to see him and, after prayer, placed his hands on him and healed him. 9 When this had happened, the rest of the sick on the island came and were cured.

Isa 53:5-6

5 But he was pierced for our transgressions, he was crushed for our iniquities; the punishment that brought us peace was upon him, and by his wounds we are healed.

6 We all, like sheep, have gone astray, each of us has turned to his own way; and the LORD has laid on him the iniquity of us all.

Luke 7:12-15

12 As he approached the town gate, a dead person was being carried out-the only son of his mother, and she was a widow. And a large crowd from the town was with her. 13 When the Lord saw her, his heart went out to her and he said, "Don't cry."

14 Then he went up and touched the coffin, and those carrying it stood still. He said,

"Young man, I say to you, get up!" 15 The dead man sat up and began to talk, and Jesus gave him back to his mother.

Acts 14:9-10

9 He listened to Paul as he was speaking. Paul looked directly at him, saw that he had faith to be healed 10 and called out, "Stand up on your feet!" At that, the man jumped up and began to walk.

Acts 5:15-16

15 As a result, people brought the sick into the streets and laid them on beds and mats so that at least Peter's shadow might fall on some of them as he passed by. 16 Crowds gathered also from the towns around Jerusalem, bringing their sick and those tormented by evil spirits, and all of them were healed.

Contact the Author L. V. Perez Jr

For speaking engagements:

(813) 541-6835

PLEN42@yahoo.com

On Facebook L.V. Perez Jr

For prayer contact me at.

Mount Tabor Bible College

P. O Box 151313

Tampa, FL 33684

Others Book by L. V. Perez Jr.

The Sixth Sense Fear

Just Believe

Suggested Reads

Suing the Devil - L.A Capdevila

Destiny to Reign-Joseph Prince

Understanding the Power and Purpose of Prayer

Dr. Myles Munroe

Good Morning Holy Spirit-Benny Hinn

You were born For This- Dr. Bruce Wilkerson

Let it Go-T.D Jakes

Ever Increasing Faith-Smith Wigglesworth

Men of The Bible- Dwight L. Moody

All of Grace-C.H Spurgeon

Battlefield of the Mind- by Joyce Meyers

Breaking Generational Curses- Marilyn Hickey

The Touch of God- Dr. Rodney H. Browne

www.ingramcontent.com/pod-product-compliance
Lightning Source LLC
Chambersburg PA
CBHW060247050426

42448CB00009B/1586